Acclaim for John Bwarie's
Nobody Walks in LA

"John Bwarie has painted a very vivid picture of the existence of everyday living in the city of Los Angeles: the automotive street life where every stop sign is a freeze frame of enjoyment and the avenues are corridors of dreams and decisions. This is the life selected by Angelenos and revealed very nicely by *Nobody Walks in LA*. A must read for everyone!"

Louis D. Alvarado, Mayor of Griffith Park

* * *

"The author's love affair with L.A. sets the tone for an insightful, amusing look at life in the city. A must read for anyone who has ever wondered why people live in Los Angeles. Bwarie does a good job of telling them why."

Dr. Doris Alvarez, Principal:
The Preuss School UCSD

* * *

"*Nobody Walks in LA* sweeps the reader along and evokes Los Angeles as we all know it."

Dr. Charles Chamberlain, Professor/Author

* * *

"Bwarie paints Los Angeles in terms of driving, where adventure looms at every red light, on every street and all of its freeways. As you travel with the author across the city, you feel his exhilaration experiencing all that the great City of Angels has to offer."

Tom LaBonge, Los Angeles City Councilmember

* * *

"*Nobody Walks in LA* is a freewheeling coming-of-age tale whose narrator cruises through his youth in the late 20th century megalopolis that is Los Angeles."

Catherine Mulholland, Author:
William Mulholland and the Rise of Los Angeles
and The Owensmouth Baby

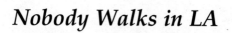

Nobody Walks in LA

Nobody Walks in LA

John Bwarie

**Twin Dolphin
Publishing**
Carlsbad, California

Published by
TWIN DOLPHIN PUBLISHING Company
Carlsbad, California.

Visit our website at
www.tdbooks.com

Library of Congress Control Number: 2002092484

ISBN 0-9668453-1-5

Cover Design by Matthew Goldman
"Ben's LA" map by Michelle Constantine

10 9 8 7 6 5 4 3 2 1
Printed in China

For Joe and Julie
who refuse to walk

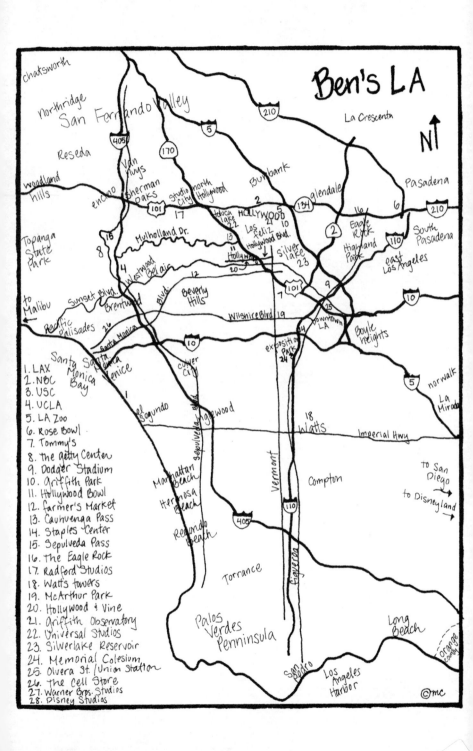

ONE

Los Angeles is alive. Driving down the Harbor Freeway through Downtown, I know that I'm part of something that is greater than I could ever know. The city's rich history gives way to a future that is mine to shape. The magic of Disneyland, the legend of Hollywood, or even the lure of the Pacific can't help but affect the way people view Los Angeles. Sometimes, I find myself being drawn into the mystique that surrounds The City of Angels. When in LA, anything is possible.

Maybe you've heard it all before in some other form. That's fine. Sure, you've had an experience here that has influenced your perception, and you did the right thing and went to try to learn more, to understand the concept of Los Angeles – great. So, you read reports, magazines, newspapers, books, or flyers demanding your understanding of the city; you've researched the region to fully grasp the meaning of the Southland. The reality of the city cannot be relayed through scientific analysis as others have tried to do, though – a person must truly live Los Angeles to understand it.

Take this one Sunday, which I have since decided was a

typically atypical LA day: light traffic, intermittent sunshine, a cultural festival of some sort happening somewhere. At the time, I was in my last year of college in San Diego, and driving back to school from a weekend in LA had become a Sunday ritual for me. But on this particular day, things were different.

My normal route of the 134 East to the 5 South had an overturned big-rig blocking the freeway right by Dodger Stadium. I didn't want to sit in that congestion, so I remained on the 101, steadily heading south. Even though sitting in traffic with Downtown in the rearview mirror is a hundred times worse than sitting in traffic with the city in full view, I still didn't want to battle other cars for the roadway. I quickly passed a pocket of slower-moving, merging cars and was on my way.

By Universal Studios, after less than 10 minutes of my habitual journey, I was already lost in thought, driving on autopilot. You know the feeling – when you're driving and all of a sudden, you look up, and you're at your destination... and you don't remember how you got there... or how you didn't get in an accident along the way. I trusted the road to keep me safe.

I'd come to LA late that Friday night and drove directly to Burbank for the 21st birthday party for Adam, one of my friends from high school. We were best friends through high school, so I had to show up, even though he was so drunk by the time I arrived that I doubt he noticed if I was there or not. His small backyard was overcrowded with people that we knew and some that nobody knew. Even in the age of email, word of mouth still fills a party that promises to have unlimited kegs.

As dawn approached, the crowd dispersed, and our core group of friends was left laughing and talking. That's the way it always ended up: Nick, Dan, Megan, Adam, Tony, Chrissie, and me – the core. We all crashed at Adam's.

I woke up at noon, and realized I only had a half hour to meet my Uncle Randy for lunch in Pasadena. He wanted to take me to eat at yet another new place he'd found: all-you-can-eat Chinese and Indian food for only $2.99 – what a deal. I sped through the light Saturday traffic to get to the restaurant on time so that I could wait another 25 minutes outside of the bright yellow hut until he got there. Throughout the mediocre meal, he relived his youth, as he often did when we would get together. And as always, he ended his long trip down the windy road of Memory Lane with, "You'll really never understand the kinds of things we did at your age." The line was not unfamiliar, but its accuracy could be debated.

After lunch, I hopped back on the 134, stopping back at Adam's house to see if he needed any help cleaning up, but he wasn't home – so much for helping him. So, I continued on to my brother's Studio City apartment to shower and change. He got home just as I was about to leave to pick up Kim. A quick hello and a "see you later," and I was on my way again.

I took Kim out for dinner and a movie, trying to transition from friends to something more. I ended up back at my brother's right after the movie... alone. Apparently, Kim wanted to "just be friends." Her loss.

I slept in on that aforementioned Sunday, and spent my first waking hours writing one of my last college essays. I left in the early afternoon to be back at my parents' house in San Diego (they had moved there from LA after I graduated high school) for dinner and then be back at school in time for one of my last study sessions ever.

The weekend had been non-stop, and I loved every minute of it, except maybe Kim and her friendship issues. I couldn't be happier about finishing up school and moving back to fast-paced LA.

The sound of a horn honking somewhere behind me broke my thought-induced trance. Startled, I tapped my brakes without thinking, then checked all three mirrors simultaneously, securing my position on the road. Behind me, I saw a truck recklessly swerve, just narrowly missing the car in the next lane. Good, I was in front of the activity; I shouldn't be held up at all, I thought.

I kept an eye on the rearview mirror, making sure that truck was not dancing across lanes – if it was, I wanted to be an eyewitness so that I could have a real LA freeway horror story to feed to my friends back at school. The truck I saw was clearly not a big-rig, nor was it a large pick-up – it was just one of those slat-sided trucks that looked like it had just driven into the big city after spending three months in California's Central Valley, caring for the world's artichoke supply.

Some of Uncle Randy's words of warning flashed through my mind: "When you're driving, remember that it's your responsibility to drive well in order to compensate for the bad drivers. And make sure you always check your mirrors to steer clear of trouble." When I first started driving, he issued it as a mandate rather than a suggestion.

As I started my journey through the Cahuenga Pass, I focused on the cars in front of me as they started to brake. I slowed, sparing plenty of room between my bumper and the car in front of me.

As I continued to monitor my rearview mirror, I caught a brief glimpse of that crazy agricultural truck. Its dark body, spotted with mud and what looked like dried lettuce, consumed my attention as it flashed between lanes as if it had no brakes.

"Come on," I said out loud in frustration. Who would take such an unwieldy vehicle on the freeway at speeds neither consistent nor considerate?

As it got closer, I saw that I had wrongfully assumed it was an empty truck. It appeared to be carrying yellow squash or something.

The forthcoming collision due to his reckless swerving was not how I wanted to conclude my weekend (or my life), so I accelerated to escape its impending assault on my small sedan. I quickly overtook a couple of cars that apparently thought it was better to let the behemoth truck pass rather than trying to out run it.

I safely stayed ahead of the truck, going well over the posted 55 miles per hour speed limit. Seeing that the truck didn't seem to be slowing nor did it seem to want to cause a collision, I realized that maybe it *was* better to slow down and just let the truck pass, as other cars had done just moments before. I considered my options in about a second.

The Arizona license plate on the car in front of me grew quickly as I approached; the Jolly Green Giant's not-so-jolly toy car closed in behind me. To the left was another car traveling at the same speed as I was - there was no way I could go left. The right lane, though, had a small, yet manageable, pocket: perfect.

I signaled, looked over my shoulder, and started to move. As is always the case, out of nowhere, a car came from the right up into my targeted lane. I swerved back into my lane as the car whizzed past. I had to get over to the right, or the reckless truck would envelop me.

The Hollywood Freeway starts to ascend again as it passes the Hollywood Bowl and approaches Vine Street, and I saw another chance to get away from the speeding truck, which was by then close enough for me to be towing. I sped up and swerved left within inches of the car in front of me. I then swung over two lanes to the right lane and took my foot off the gas... and finally exhaled.

The speeding truck continued to climb the urban "mountain," the short ascent having no effect on its speed. Its brake lights shone bright against the dirty truck like giant gemstones suspended in the La Brea Tar Pits. The load was now obvious as he passed me: lemons.

I started to accelerate with caution and the lemon truck still in sight, not yet crested the small incline. With the truck ahead of me, I assumed it would be smooth sailing. Maybe I was too much like my dad in that way: "almost out of sight, already out of mind."

Before I realized what happened, the lemon truck erratically swerved out of its lane. Cars honked as it skidded across the lanes, and then tipped over, crashing down on the freeway. I heard the screeches and scraping that followed without thinking of anything except, "That can't be good for those people up there." No one else was in direct danger of hitting the truck; the cars around it had cleared away and maintained a distance. I think everyone thought something like this might happen and figured distance would be the best combative maneuver. This would've been true if I had sped up and passed the truck.

With all these events taking place within a few moments, I didn't immediately realize what had happened. At first, I was shocked at the truck's tipping over and spilling its load of lemons. But those lemons didn't just spill, they poured. Bouncing down the freeway, they came, the wrath of lemons unleashed upon the innocent freeway and its travelers. Bushels and bushels of lemons attacked the drivers in their path. Unrelenting, the lemons kept coming; the bed of the truck had been deeper than I expected.

The lemons bounced against the cars and over each other. As they came closer, I tried to swerve to the right, possibly avoiding the brunt of their roll, but I wasn't fast enough. And it wasn't like a wall of lemons crashed down and covered the car; just a small swell surrounded the tires, making movement difficult. The lemons started to gather around the car as they continued to roll from the spill.

The acidic lemons attacked me. Like an oil slick, they enveloped my car not to the point of total destruction, but to the point of immobility. I couldn't go backward because the bulk of them was behind me, and I couldn't go forward because the lemons were making the road slick with a film that made my tires spin. I was stuck.

The afternoon sun shone as bright as the acidic road. We had to wait for the police and fire department to "rescue" us from the lemons; they had us walk from our cars to the shoulder as they located and used snow shovels to gather the escaped lemons and free our cars. I was one of 29 victims of a citrus explosion.

I'm sure some people sued because they were wrongfully delayed, though no car showed any true damage besides the flipped truck. Traffic was backed up all the way to the 405 as they cleared the spill, which probably made a lot of people pretty upset, or just react as they do every other day.

I thought it was amazing, though. True, I was two hours late to my parents' house, which delayed my study session, but what better lesson is there than learning how to survive disaster.

LA is full of potential disasters; if you dwell on the negative side, you'll be eaten alive.

Well, had that been the turning point between LA and me, I might not be here talking to you now. I could have gotten discouraged with the whole freeway system, cried out for the "good old days" of the Red Cars, and retreated to San Diego. That's what I'm told people do – hell, that *is* what my parents did.

See, most people just go along with the crowd. The herd moves right along, everyone tailgating the person they're following, sometimes practically locking bumpers so the follower doesn't even need to think. Conformity leads to collision.

I was born into a conformist society, but by no means am I a conformist. And that became very clear when I got to high school and again in college. It's not that I am a non-conformist, but as I started to develop my own ideas about the way things should be, I started doing things my way. I didn't change the way I looked to reject the norm, but instead, I like to think that I worked within that norm to change its meaning. And what is normal, anyway? Right?

For me, normal is living in the real world, Los Angeles; working for a major corporation but being hired without an interview; driving hundreds of miles a week to get to work, to a friend, or to think. Some would consider that abnormal, but I see it as almost commonplace.

Sometimes I cause the change; sometimes the change happens to me.

TWO

Sure, you don't encounter a lemon spill every weekend in LA, but something out of the ordinary should be expected: out of the ordinary becomes ordinary. My mother used to say that things happened to me because I was young and adventurous. But even as an adult, the adventures have come to be expected because of my existence in LA.

A few years after the burst of lemons on the 101 and not too long ago from today, I had a memorable experience so out of the ordinary, it helped define who I am today. Well, it may not have been the specific day that actually changed my life, but from that day forward, I consciously knew things had changed. Either way, I blame that day...

It was like the first shot from one of its movies. LA opened up before me as I drove from the Valley, over the Cahuenga Pass, and into the heart of the city, a route I had taken since before I even started driving. (And at the time, I was still leery of produce trucks coming over that small hill.) Finished with school and off of work, I drove into the familiar unknown for an adventure. I've always looked at life as an adventure, and there's no better place to have one than in Los Angeles. And you can't really successfully search out an adventure; no, you just have to let it happen to you as you experience the city.

In LA, people have always gone about their lives in ways that have caught the attention of many. Some who have taken notice are fellow residents of the vast metropolis; others, outsiders, look into the city as if it's contained within a Sylvia Plath-like bell jar. Some present accurate portrayals of an unforgiving economy, a resentful environment, or a phenomenon known simply as Hollywood. Stories have been fathomed, and anecdotes, circulated worldwide. Screenplays have been revised (and revised and revised and revised), still not quite capturing the true essence that the studio wants. As third graders, we write fledgling reports for social studies classes when studying the local history unit on pueblos with a trip to Olvera Street. And daily, the people starving for attention chase their dreams, writing signs of sympathy (or any other number of billboards, flyers, posters, and vehicles) for all of LA to read. Starving artists.

Only too late – in high school – did I recognize that LA

8

was not just the image of Hollywood glamour, either. Beyond the scandals, real estate, facelifts, money, and upper-class stereotypes, a population exists of poor people, regular people: immigrants, day-laborers, middle and working class families, single moms struggling to make it work, and people who *do* care what's east of Downtown. Beyond the Hollywood Hills, beyond the estates of Pasadena and Palos Verdes, beyond beachfront property, houses in the hills, homes so far north they are Santa Barbara's, and beyond the limitations of a segregated city, sprawls the Union of Los Angeles: the complete LA. Multifaceted is an understatement – LA is an atomic reaction of possibilities.

See, for me, the city was - and still is - full of potential. It's not that it holds lots of opportunities for me or you or anyone striving to find those opportunities right now, but the actual city, itself, has the potential to flourish beyond its current status. Don't get me wrong – LA is far from perfect. But it's like the boulder my chemistry teacher conjured in explaining potential energy: it's at a precarious position on the top of a hill, and a slight movement in the right direction will send it on its downhill course of releasing that stored energy. That's about the only principle in chemistry that I really understood. And that's LA in a nutshell: if you crack it the right way, the potential released will be the greatest adventure.

So, I was driving on the 101 South towards the city's center – my windows down, my CD player blaring. Relatively smog-free, the blue sky and the low-lying clouds framed the downtown skyline. The hovering clouds bore a striking resemblance to the painted backdrop on the Universal Studios tour that *Jaws* was filmed against. The city council didn't have to use special effects to lure tourists that day.

As I cruised along, my cell phone rang. Normally, I wouldn't answer my cell while driving, but the Caller ID flashed "Calhoun, Cynthia." Cindi was hanging out for the summer before starting back at her graduate program at UCLA. We used to date but at that point, and by her prompting, were "just friends."

"Cindi, where were you when I called?"

"Hello to you, too. I was getting my beauty sleep. And now, I'm on the Freeway heading toward *your* Valley.

"Oh, too bad, I'm heading out of it. I wish you would've called earlier."

"Sorry. I'm off to my cousin's for that barbeque I told you about, but I'll be done around 5:30. You in the car?"

"No, I'm taking a walk. Yes, I'm in the car. And actually, I'm heading towards your area – I'm on the Hollywood Freeway now."

"Me, too. But heading north. Wouldn't be cool if we saw each other?" She laughed. "Where you going, though?"

"I'm just driving into Downtown; I'm gonna do some research at the Central Library. Then, I'm off to my grandparents' for dinner."

"Oh, that library's cool. Good luck finding parking."

"I know."

"Hey, maybe we can meet around the Los Feliz area after my thing - maybe grab coffee or something before you have to go to your grandparents'."

"Maybe. But I don't think you'll make it by the time I have to leave for Pasadena."

"Didn't you hear me? I said it's over around five. It's only 2:30 – that gives you three hours to do whatever, and then we can hang out for a little while before you have to head to your grandparents'. Hey, you ever notice how the Silver Lake exit is more gray than silver?"

"Maybe you didn't hear *me*? I said I was going to my grandparents'. You know the ones; we've dropped things off at their house a few times. They live in that historic bungalow off Mountain on Chester Street. As for dinner, four o'clock is a late for them." What is it that makes grandparents eat dinner so early? "I'm just coming up on the Sunset exit, which is more of dusk, by the way, if you ask me."

"Are you mocking me?" Her overly exaggerated self-defense was one of her strong suits.

"No, no. I'd never dream of it. What lane are you in,

though? Maybe we *can* see each other today."

"I'm in the third lane over – why? Ben, what are you thinking? Is this gonna be safe?" Cindi seemed to be catching on.

"Listen. Quick, get in the left lane – that's where I am. I just passed Sunset. Whose car you driving?"

"Mine. I don't know about you sometimes, Ben."

"Well, I should be able to spot that eye sore from my side of the freeway... and what don't you know?"

"Just that I can't believe you sometimes. What am I saying - *most* of the time. You have a real life with a full-time job and everything, and then you do all this volunteering all over the place – a real citizen. And yet, with all of that, you *still* have these really random moments – which, I guess, aren't so random with you."

"Whatever. Everyone's got their own quirks, not that my randomness is a quirk. Now come on, where are you? My arm's out the window." I was getting excited at the idea of an encounter with Cindi on the Hollywood Freeway.

"I'm just passing Melrose."

"Okay – it should be any second now. Brace yourself."

"Alright. I can't believe we're doing this."

I spotted her red Explorer come around the bend right at that very instant; and I think she waved. I honked and waved, but we never really made eye contact.

"Did you see me?" I said, laughing at the absurdity of the rendezvous.

"Yeah, I think so," she giggled. "You're too much."

"Well, thank you; thank you very much. My work is now complete. Maybe I'll see you later tonight"

"Okay. Well, have fun at your grandparents. And oh, if you feel like eating again at ten – you know, five hours after you eat dinner – call me. Maybe we can go to Tommy's or something." Cindi was one of the only girls I knew that liked going to Tommy's, but I was intrigued by the 'or something'.

"Why don't you call me and check in when you're done; I'll have my cell on. Who knows where I'll be."

"Okay, seeya. "

I smiled as I headed down the freeway, thinking of how absurd, yet strikingly normal, the previous few minutes had been. Creativity and determination will release the city's potential. And the fact that most folks have cell phones now doesn't hurt things, either.

THREE

Just around Silver Lake Boulevard (which lately *did* appear more gray than silver), red brake lights blinded me. Traffic always started to slow here as it headed into the Downtown Four-Level, the intersection of two of LA's major freeways: the 101 and the 110. I wasn't surprised, nor did the slowing to practical non-movement bother me. I wasn't in any hurry; you can't rush the city.

Traffic in the right lanes was moving better than the "fast" lane, which I had chosen. I put on my blinker and started moving right. It never fails that the right lane, the "slow lane," moves faster during traffic times than the other lanes. It was the work of the Gods. The Freeway Gods.

See, most drivers in LA are unaware that freeway traffic is not determined by too many cars, Cal-Trans roadwork, or the daily, high-speed police chase. No, the opposing delays or speeding that occur on Southern California freeways are directly related to the Freeway Gods' fickle moods.

A deity system, not unlike the gods of ancient times, governs the roads. But this is a different kind of Greece: even Aristophanes would have trouble conjuring up a more extreme set of divine beings. Every freeway has it's own deity, the major freeways having the major Gods. The Gods have no awe-inspiring or even witty names that represent their personality – just practical, no-nonsense, efficient names like God of the 101 or Goddess of the 210. Most are decent enough, too – practically human. A couple of the major Gods, though, have some ego issues, hence traffic congestion.

Take, for instance, the God of the 405: he is best likened to a 14-year-old boy. He has no real understanding of driving and likes to see things fall into chaos or even destroyed. What distinguishes this God is that he gets pleasure out of seeing others delayed, knowing exactly how to create congestion. It's not the cars traveling to LAX that create the jammed 405; it's the God of the 405's fiendish, mismanaged aggression. He's still a kid with his magnifying glass, reveling with each fried ant. On top of that, I think he has a pet that he either doesn't feed or let out to "go." The dastardly creature roams the Sepulveda Pass, wreaking havoc. With this understood, it is slightly comprehensible why there's always traffic on the 405, especially heading into or out of the Valley.

Conversely, the Goddess of the 2 is a flower-loving, tree-hugging spirit of the earth. The small freeway that goes from Silver Lake north to the Angeles National Forest rarely has congestion, and traffic usually travels well above the speed limit. This Goddess just lets things flow... for the most part.

Some drivers will argue that, in fact, they do get stuck in traffic on the 2 South heading into LA or merging onto the 5. This happens because the most powerful Freeway God, God of the 5, is taking control of things and not letting any of the other freeways have their way. The Gods cannot – or will not - compromise, and the resulting traffic is standing proof.

Actually, the one common attribute between the whole assemblage of Freeway Gods is that they all want their way to be the right way. Why wouldn't they: the road most traveled is the road most regarded, right? And unfortunately for the drivers, the Gods could care less who their quibbling affects. No offerings can be made to the Gods to sway them in any direction; no sacrifice can be offered to appease them. As a driver, I've just accepted that traffic is the Freeway Gods at work.

The Freeway Gods control the movements – the arrivals, the departures, the stalls, the speeds – of the motorists that traverse the roads. No matter what a driver hopes to achieve in leaving early or late to avoid traffic, if the Gods are not willing, the roads will be filled. Randomly, if a motorist leaves extra time and the Gods are in a good mood, their arrival might allow them to have more free time than they know what to do with. A transition from the 101 to the 110 might be crowded one minute and open the next. Motorists have no control – it's up to the Gods. And if two motorists leave the same point at the same time and take two different routes to reach the same destination, even if one takes a shortcut or the other drives fast, it's ultimately up to the Gods to see who arrives first. On a good day, they arrive at the same time.

Since I wasn't in a rush to get downtown, I let the roads - the Freeway Gods - guide me. I knew I didn't want to be a pawn in their game and battle with other cars, so I got off the freeway and let the Gods of the 101 and the 110 squabble over who was to have the cars that afternoon. I turned off at Alvarado Street, heading into the city. Apparently, I wasn't the only one who thought of avoiding the wrath of the Freeway Gods.

FOUR

I waited at the top of the off-ramp while slow-moving cars merged into Alvarado's congested lanes. A true palette of cars awaited movement on the off-ramp: a late model jalopy with a mismatched, rust-color door, a brand new Toyota 4Runner with a gleaming black finish, an old, dirt-colored pickup from the '50s, and a few-year-old BMW in fairly decent shape, minus the dent in the bumper. This off-ramp was LA.

If accepted, the sprawling City of Los Angeles can give a person their identity. Live long enough in any city, and you'll become part of its presence, and in turn, that presence will become part of you. But because of its dynamic nature and diverse history, Los Angeles, stands as a great influence; LA shapes its residents and the world.

14

Words alone are proof enough of LA's impact on the world. "Los Angeles English" is the version of American English that is accent-free. People in Los Angeles speak a certain way; and since the dawn of Hollywood, the expansive media that has shaped the world's speech is distinctively LA. I'm not saying it's the *right* way; it's just *the* way. So, even if I go Back East to visit relatives in Boston or New York, they're still the ones with the accent. And while there, if I turn on the TV to the local news, their newscasters speak in LA English as though they've navigated the freeways and lived off Dodger Dogs and year-long sunshine.

For some, it might be difficult to understand how the city makes people who they are. Even now, after going to college and returning to LA with my degree, I still am learning from the city. I can zip around from here to there: lunch on the Westside, dinner on the Eastside. And as I travel, I continue to develop. The city persists and thrives because of its dynamic nature, and it's always kind to its benefactors, its supporters, its founders, its citizens.

The signal at the bottom of the ramp turned green again, and I finally made it onto Alvarado heading south towards McArthur Park, towards the heart of the city. I was finally on my way, and this time, for real. Sometimes it takes a couple tries to really get going, but once you do, it's hard to stop. The city won't let you.

FIVE

And just as soon as I got started – again – I stopped: a red light a block from the freeway. On the corner to my right, a liquor store advertised specials on cigarettes, lottery tickets, and cold 12-paks of Corona. Peering inside the open door from the right lane, I saw a traditional liquor store and immediately noticed how dark it was.

"Will you look at that," I said out loud to myself. "I can't believe how much they're charging for a bottle of JaNece Reserve wine now." I usually only talk aloud to myself when I am sure of something, like when billboards are written in poor grammar ("SUDDENLY, your alone: A fragrance for women"). "And they have the cases stacked too high and too close to the door"; I knew that for a fact.

You see, I was born in a liquor store. My parents owned one in the Valley from before the time my older brother was born. When James cried his way into the world, a banner went up behind the counter announcing that "it" was a boy. Pictures soon accompanied this sign, dwarfing those already tiny bottles of liquor kept behind the cashier. Everyone knows that pregnancy and drinking don't mix, but apparently, baby pictures and liquor do.

It was actually in the aisles of that store that my brother first experienced crawling and gurgling. When he was teething, my parents gave him beef jerky to gnaw, and when he was learning to walk, they made sure he did so down a wine or beer aisle and not one with the Roedierer Crystal or Dom Perignon or Chivas Regal. And it was about this time when the idea of a second child was conceived.

And when my mother was pregnant with me, she did things as would a veteran pregnant woman. She even went so far as to go to Las Vegas with only one month before I was due. And during this weekend getaway with my dad, the big event happened: she met Michael Landon. My mother's favorite experience of that year was not my birth, but her encounter with "Little Joe," "Charles Ingalls," Michael Landon. And every time we saw an extremely pregnant woman, she would tell me that story.

"I was reading a magazine near the pool at The Mirage. And I noti—"

"Were you wearing a maternity swimsuit?" I asked, impishly, the first time she told the story.

"No," she said abruptly, seeming offended that I interrupted her *Highway to Heaven*, out-of-body experience. "I noticed him across the pool. So, I gathered you up and waddled over to him. I put out my hand and said, 'Mr. Landon, I just want to thank you for putting on such wonderful programming for me and my family to watch.' He was polite, and said 'you're welcome,' and then I walked back to my *Family Circle* magazine." She would then explain that she had no need to stay and try to talk; she reacted to him as a real person.

When she returned to LA, she worked in the store until the day I was born. While standing sideways in the freezer aisle filling in the Häagen Dazs ice cream cups, she started getting stomach pains. She went to the little office in back, which had only enough space for a desk and my brother's playpen (where he was napping). My dad had gone on a delivery to Paramount Studios to deliver a "Thank You" bottle of champagne to the *Star Trek* executives, so my mother was running the store.

So, my mother was in the backroom with her contractions and a sleeping toddler, and my dad was gone. Back in the store, the only other employee working was a high school student who was the son of the owners of the neighboring shoe store – my parents believed in helping out those around you. But with the labor my mom was doing, he was no help.

My mother was basically alone and had no one to call. No, there were plenty of people to call - just no one that could come to her. She called her mother who was no help because, by that time, she had already "given up" driving the freeways (and this was well before they really got congested), so she remained a nervous 20 minutes away in Pasadena. My mom was without a sister, but even all her sister-like friends had gone to Glendale that afternoon, at her urging, for the engagement party of yet another couple from their group of friends. So, my mom said she coped as best she could, abating the pain with her short, deep breaths. I envision an altered *I Love Lucy* episode.

My dad came back about 15 minutes later, ready to tell a story about how he was stopped by a woman who wanted to discuss gift deliveries, but my mother had already made her way to the front of the store. Waiting with her purse over her shoulder, her two-year-old grasped in one hand, and her stomach held in the other, my mom made my dad close the store. He complied, but not before putting a handmade sign in the window that read "closed due to birth." Beaming, he drove his brown Toyota station wagon – with his family piled inside – to the hospital.

My grandmother finally made it to the hospital before I arrived because of my grandfather's expertise in driving the post-rush hour freeways (and thanks to the Freeway Gods, who seem to go to bed early on most nights). Later that night, when a call was made to the post-engagement-party party, a loud cheer was heard as the second son's name was announced: Benjamin. And if you were to drive down Van Nuys Boulevard the following day, you probably would have noticed the obscenely large banner hanging above the "closed" sign in the window. It was not advertising a weekly special on Coke or cartons of Marlboro's. This sign was advertising me: "It's a Boy...again."

So, I, like my brother before me, spent my first years learning about life from the inside of a liquor store. The faux wood paneling and the deep burgundy and orange carpets were as much my playground as the Studio City Park. Even today, the smell of a cigar humidor, the chill of a giant, glass-doored refrigerator, or the sound of a breaking bottle of wine transport me back to the days when those were the components of my adventures.

My parents' store was typical of the 1950s – but in the '80s. It was a family operation, and everyone helped out: my aunt, my uncles, my cousins, and even my grandmother until she was 89 years old.

As James and I got older, we helped out, too, doing the menial jobs that only a four- or five-year-old could do. We were responsible for getting all the candy that had fallen behind the candy rack by lying on our little bellies and sticking our nimble arms under the rack and into the unknown, dust-covered crevices of a liquor store shelf. We also dusted all the bottom shelf bottles and organized the loose packs of cigarettes behind the counter. But as a toddler, one of the best jobs was to clean all the freezer and refrigerator case windows. That was great! Or at least, that's what our parents convinced us.

But it wasn't all work at the liquor store. My parents were firm believers in "family time," and one way to experience it was through family dinners, which we had every night in some form or another. When my dad could not take a break to come home to eat with us, we would eat dinner at the store. Mom would cook at home and bring the food to the small store. Cars driving down Van Nuys on one of those nights might have caught a glimpse of a small family sitting at a folding table in the front window just beyond a banner crying out that California Lottery Tickets were "now available." Eating together was an important fixture of family life, even if that shared meal was not in the home.

I'm not kidding when I say it was no ordinary store, but a family working a store is no new concept. What continued to make my youth in this store interesting were the things that only a fulltime employee or frequent customer might see. And this doesn't even include the things that happened just outside of the store: occasional filmings of *Hill Street Blues*, a drunk driver carefully plowing through the front window, people lining the street to see the Olympic Torch pass in 1984. The things on the inside were just as interesting, if not more so.

Most of the important events in my life were connected to the store. Family Christmas parties, birthday parties, and even class fieldtrips all happened in my dad's store. A customer coming into to buy orange juice might end up singing happy birthday or showing up in the background of family pictures. And the guests at these parties were whom you would expect: employees, sales reps, other merchants from the shopping center, and my grandmother, just for a moment, when she would take short breaks from her work to make an appearance at a party. I knew no different, so I assumed that every child received free samples and "pick anything you want from this aisle" as gifts. I guess I lied: I wasn't just born in the store; I was raised in it.

The location of the store in Sherman Oaks – just over the hill from Beverly Hills and just minutes away from the

Hollywood Hills, Studio City, and Encino – affected the clientele, and in turn, what we were able to do in the store. My dad would sometimes mention refusing service to customers if they were already drunk (he called them "reeking"), but more lasting are the memories of the rich and famous coming into the store, or at least my dad retelling stories of such encounters at the dinner table.

Coming home later than he had planned, Dad would walk in announcing, "Well, I was just about to walk out the door to come home when Tyne Daily came in the store. She wanted help with a case of wine, so I had to stay." Between bites of food, he would he would explain how the producers from *The Love Boat* called up and order engraved bottles of wine for the cast or that his friends at Paramount were ordering holiday gifts for all of their holiday film stars. His customers were so assorted - and so LA - that whenever we would watch TV, without fail, my dad would read the credits and say, "That's our customer."

"Yep, he's our customer," he would say as the Director of Photography for an episode of *The Cosby Show* would flash on the screen. Whether we were watching *Cheers* or a new movie from John Hughes, one of my dad's customers would be in the credits. And even later, when we no longer had that store in the Valley, we'd watch an episode of *ER* or *Law and Order*, and he would say, "Oh, hey, she used to be our customer. She used to come in and buy –" and he would recall exactly what kind of wine they bought or the brand of cigars they would smoke. Dad kept us all up-to-date on which film editors used to be on *LA Law* and had since moved on to another one of Steven Bochco's projects. He knew his customers. And they knew his store and service was like no other store in LA.

When I was old enough, I, too, began to help out serving these customers. At eight, I started doing more than just the dusting and cleaning and "little kid" jobs; I started working behind the counter, learning to run the register and ringing up sales. I would ring up candy bars and soft drinks; snack foods and cigarettes; vodka and Champagne. I was not completely alone at the cash register checking IDs: my dad or another employee always looked over my shoulder. I felt like I wasn't given the opportunity to shine as a clerk while someone watched over me, so I memorized the prices of all the products in the liquor store to prove my capability. I showed them.

I was lucky enough to be paid a dollar for every hour I worked, and I really had to work hard for it. I learned to count back change without just wadding up the person's change, but actually counting it back starting with the coins and then the bills. By the time I was 11, I was on my way to a successful retail career and a life free of stress.

My dad sold the store when I was 14, and we moved along to the next business: a store in the mall. Not until I was older did I realize what I had had at my fingertips for all those years. Later, when classmates of mine would talk about pony kegs and cases of beer and mixed drink ingredients, I knew what they were talking about from experience... and how much they cost. And when they would brag about their fake IDs, I could pick apart the little details that proved them fake. So, when I encountered full-blown, underage drinking and partying at college, I was not fazed; and I was sure that it wasn't for me. Because I grew up in a liquor store, those kinds of things were not new and exciting to me, even when I was "free" in college.

My father's liquor store drove me to find even newer and more exciting things to try when I reached the age of exploration. I wanted to do things; I wanted to build things, go on adventures with friends, and spend the money I had earned and saved since I started working at four-years-old. When the time came, I wasn't going to look back and rekindle that loving relationship I had with alcohol and tobacco – there was nothing they could give me that they hadn't already.

Back at the corner where I was stopped, I was lost in memories of a liquor store youth, patiently waiting for the light to turn green.

SIX

I intensely watched the cross-traffic light turn yellow, preparing myself to be released from the gates. When the gate finally opened and my light turned green, I apparently didn't move fast enough: the car behind me hit me. Like the impatient customer that is never satisfied no matter how fast you go, this driver accelerated before I even had a chance to take my foot off the brake.

"Oh, crap. Just what I need."

Frustrated that my car might have some damage, I cautiously pulled through the intersection and stopped on the other side at the curb. The attacker followed. I warily got out of my car and, thankfully, saw that no damage was done to my car. I finally exhaled. The other driver, a petite, young woman with blonde hair, seemed extremely distraught as she noticed a slight crumple in her bumper. She sat back down in her older model Mercedes and just stared at nothing.

"Don't worry about it," I said. "There doesn't seem to be anything wrong with my car."

"Okay. Okay." She said in a slight southern accent but without composure. She looked like she was in her late twenties as she pulled the hair off her face. Her subtle features reflected the day's bright sun.

"Are you okay?" I asked, trying to comfort the stranger. I was not thrilled with the idea of being outside of my car in an area prone to crime, but the woman didn't look like she was okay. It wouldn't hurt me to stand there a few more moments until she gained composure, I thought. At that moment, as if on cue, she started bawling.

"It's okay," I said. "No real damage was done. It was just a little tap. Don't even worry about it."

My words came out uncomfortably as she nodded, wiping her eyes. Her hair fell again across half her face. Looking up at me, she softly she said her first coherent sentence to me:

"Do you have a cell phone that I could possibly use?"

I was slowly connecting with this mysterious girl. If she had asked me for money at that moment, or even my car, I might have given it to her. It was the least I could do, for such a woman, who seemed out of place.

I went back to my car, got the phone, and made sure I locked the car before I walked back to hers. Who knows how long I would be away from the car.

I walked up to her car and handed her my phone, telling her it was no problem. She took the phone and started dialing. She put the phone up to her ear and then looked at me as if to say, "can I have some privacy for a minute please." Seeing the pain in her eyes, I turned and walked a couple of steps to the sidewalk.

I glanced up and down the street a few times, then across to buildings of Downtown. "Why did I get off the freeway this time?" I thought to myself. I looked back and smiled. She smiled back. She started talking louder and then closed her door. Privacy – okay, I could handle that.

For the few minutes that she spoke, she winced and made faces. I figured she was upset over what had happened and was talking to her mom or a boyfriend or someone. She seemed to say her good-byes rather quickly and with a frown. I should've known by that point something wasn't right with the mysterious beauty. I should have realized it when she hit me, but I was easily distracted that day.

Before I was able to approach the driver's side of the car to retrieve my phone, she screeched away from the curb, leaving only the resounding echoes of her speed.

"Hey! My phone!" I ineffectively yelled at her as she sped away. I saw her window open, and without slowing, she tossed my phone out the window as she turned right at the next street. I ran to my car, fumbled for the keys to unlock the door, dropped them twice, and then finally sat down and started my car.

I sped after her, but when I turned down that first street, all I saw was a woman sitting on her stoop, grinning. Realizing the chances of finding her on the streets of LA, I went back to where the phone was flung.

I got out and picked up the mangled phone from the gutter where it was rejected. I pushed the power button on the traumatized phone. It turned on but the screen was all scrambled, not to mention growing a crack down the middle of the entire phone. "Dammit!"

I got back into my car and slammed the door. I threw the phone down on the floor next to me. It beeped. "Dammit," I snarled between my teeth, irritated at the unexpected hassle (and cost) of a broken phone.

Swerving back onto Alvarado, livid at what just happened, I clenched my teeth. She hadn't tried to rip me off or con me – she just was completely inconsiderate. "What an ass," my flexed jaw contained my rage.

Almost instantly, I hit another red light. "ARGH!" I yelled, stopping just behind the crosswalk line. I hit my steering wheel with my fist and then looked down at my crippled phone. When I looked through my windshield again, an old, leathered woman was walking past in the crosswalk. Like a teapot, she was short and stout, and her dark complexion seemed to absorb the sun. She grasped an over-sized purse – a duffle bag, really – in one hand and pulled a yellow wagon with a miniature mutt of dog in it with the other. She looked at me and smiled; she only had one visible tooth.

"Oh - my – god," I said slowly between my clamped teeth as they formed a smile. I couldn't hold back an embarrassed explosion of laughter when I realized she had dressed her dog in a dainty tuxedo. I felt bad for the woman; I felt worse for the dog.

The light turned green, and I immediately took off up one of the earthquake-formed hills on Alvarado without looking back. It was time to go before being stopped again.

After a drive-by with Cindi and a broken phone resulting from a damage-less collision, I wasn't sure what would happen next. What I was sure of was that I was living in LA. You can't change where you come from, but the choice of where you go is all yours.

SEVEN

I had only been driving for about an hour that day and already had had the adventure I wasn't looking for. And now, I had the aggravation of both a broken phone and social isolation. My frustration with my phone subsided when I remembered I had reluctantly purchased phone insurance as part of my coverage. Social isolation, I later realized, was not just because of a communication blackout.

With a calm mind, I figured I'd just drive over to The Cell Store and get it replaced – I had plenty of time. The adventure was over; now, I was on a mission.

I had purchased the phone and the calling plan from a virtually unknown company because their rates were the lowest in the city. But as part of the deal – the catch – I had to go to one of their few stores for any service issues, and at that point, the only store I knew of was on the Westside in Santa Monica. As I came upon Third Street, I impulsively turned off Alvarado and headed west away from downtown to cross the city to get my phone fixed.

Just after passing Our Lady of the Angels Medical Center, I slowed as I descended towards Rampart. On my left, the grounds keeper of the church was walking to his car, having just locked the gate. Sunday services at the church across the street had come and gone. I waved.

It wasn't my church, but I was connected to it. Before marrying into Catholicism, my mom had been Orthodox. Her side of the family still was, and this was the church that we went to for her family's services: baptisms, funerals, weddings, and special masses. An Orthodox Christian (not to be confused with an Orthodox Jew) is practically a Catholic but without the Pope, among other things. Thirteen years of Catholic school elucidated this point with multiple investigations of the Church's split in A.D. 1054.

And even though it wasn't my faith, I sometimes went

to that Orthodox church as much as I went to my own Catholic church. To me, Orthodoxy and Catholicism were basically the same; someone, somewhere, just needed to say so officially. But that's a whole other issue entirely.

Anyway, upon passing the church, I decided, instead of taking Third, to take Wilshire all the way west through the Miracle Mile to Santa Monica. It would be faster and more scenic, and I could drive it in about 20 minutes.

As I waited to turn left at Rampart, I immediately thought of Tommy's, which was just down Rampart, but to the right about five blocks at Beverly. I don't think you can live in LA and not know about Tommy's World Famous Hamburgers. It's as much a part of LA's culinary history as Philippe's for French dips or Pink's for hot dogs. To tourists, I think, having a Tommy's Burger is like having a cheese steak sandwich at Sam's in Philadelphia or a Gino's deep-dish pizza in Chicago – it's a regional delicacy. And unlike LA restaurants like The Original Pantry or El Cholo, Tommy's is just a shack with an international reputation.

As a child, having a Tommy's Burger is an experience that I shared with my dad every time we were in the area of Rampart and Beverly and, then later, one I shared with my friends. The confined, little stand that started it all (now an island in the parking lot of the expanded eatery) has enough history for an entire book, not to mention the best burgers. But this reputation had always been a bit misleading, though.

See, eating a Tommy's Burger is the best burger-eating *experience*. The grease-soaked wrapper and the oozing chili define the Burger, as does the unchanging way they've been prepared on the same grill used for over 50 years. Other burgers in LA are just as tasty, if not better, but the consumption experience leaves something to be desired. In-N-Out has the freshest fast food burger, by far; but what you get when you eat at the original Tommy's cannot be recreated – that makes it the best.

This powerful feeling is so unique that even eating a Tommy's burger at one of its recently opened "other" locations is never as great as eating at the original stand that my dad ate at when he was a teenager. The reputation of Tommy's – the experience connected with eating a Tommy's Burger – makes it world famous. When you eat standing up at the street-side shack with cars rushing by on Rampart, a transformation occurs. It must be something in the chili or on the grill.

This feeling also connects everyone who has ever eaten a Tommy's Burger. It's the idea that you can say, "Hey, you going to Tommy's?" and people, even if it is not mealtime or if they've just eaten, will say, "sure."

When I started going to St. Vincent High School, Tommy's played a crucial role in the educational process. Teachers would pick Tommy's up for club meetings and even for "class". And while working in the school's theater on stage crew, our only full-day Saturday crew session tradition was to break as a group when going to Tommy's. Tommy's has a legacy that goes beyond the actual hamburger itself.

People recognize the power of the Burger, which is why when you drive through LA, you see Tomy's, Tommi's, Tommies, and Thommy's and innumerable others trying to capture the enchantment that surrounds the original Tommy's. And for me, the epitome of this magic took place on the night before my high school graduation.

Our Baccalaureate Mass on Friday night preceded the actual commencement exercises of the following morning. All of us seniors drove our own cars (or carpooled) that night, as we had to be at school an hour before our parents were to arrive. Then, after the Mass, we had a reception with catered food. At about 10 p.m., after the reception had all but ended, a small group of us were standing around. No one really wanted to go home, which, for each of us, was in a different part of the city, so someone suggested going to Tommy's.

"One last time as high schoolers," someone said, so we each got into our individual cars and drove over to the original Tommy's. We practically filled the already crowded lot across the street when we pulled in and still had to cross Rampart and stand in line. When we finally reached the other side, we saw about 30 other guys from our class who had had the same idea: commemorate that turning point in life at Tommy's.

Tommy's is uniquely LA, no matter how many copies try to imitate the original. Sometimes, after going to my mom's church for a holiday or some special occasion, a group of us will drive the few blocks to Tommy's for a ceremonial burger. Tommy's is the closest thing to a religious experience in the fast food world. Sure, you could go to the golden calf of the Golden Arches, but with over 50 years of grease from serving LA, the original Tommy's Burger is no false god.

EIGHT

Turning away from Tommy's with the knowledge that I might possibly be returning to the hallowed Los Angeles shrine that evening with Cindi, I turned on Rampart heading towards Wilshire. I passed apartments on the wide, treeless street with people on the stoops preceded by barely apparent patches of grass. A man was yelling at two women as they tried to carry a new couch into an apartment. Little girls wore dresses and cowboy boots as they walked along the avenue with their mothers, perhaps coming from or going to church. Other children played in front of their apartments ignoring the traffic less than ten feet away. This seemed to be a completely different childhood than I experienced just 14 miles and a few years away in the Valley.

LA's San Fernando Valley is still where I call home. Just 20 minutes from the skyscrapers of Downtown, the beaches of Santa Monica, and the Rose Bowl in Pasadena, Studio City remains the center of my LA. I live just between the Hollywood Freeway, the Ventura Freeway, and the San Diego Freeway – a very convenient location, indeed. And as the battles continue to rage over which part of LA is best or deserves the most recognition – Eastside or Westside, the valley or the basin – I can happily remain neutral and proudly claim, "I live in the Valley, but I'm from Los Angeles."

Though I will gladly reply, "The Valley," to questions of origin, I would not call myself a Valley Boy. Although it's, like, totally cool to, like, be from the Valley; it's like, ya' know, difficult to, ya' know, like, to live up to, like, the image, like, you see in, like, the movies. I admit it: I've shopped in the Sherman Oaks Galleria, a setting used for movies *Valley Girl* and *Fast Times at Ridgemont High*. You know, it was torn down; I think local civic leaders trying to eradicate the reputation it brought to the region thought this would be the answer. Replaced by office buildings, now, the site never seems to be completely rented – that's what happens when you demolish a landmark, an identity.

I identify with the Valley as a staging ground for relating to the rest of LA. You've got to start somewhere, and my parents chose the Valley for me.

I grew up in a house that sat at the convergence of two dead end streets. Quite an unusual situation in terms of city planning, our street was only three houses long, and the street that feeds directly into it had a different name. Basically, our street never appeared on maps, and when I would give directions, I would never actually refer to my street's name. The resulting neighborhood was very quiet and served my purposes as the arena for my wild escapades.

Unlike the kids on Rampart, I lived in a neighborhood conducive for children to be playing in the street without the fear of cars interrupting games or running over our Big Wheels. The next-door neighbors' son, Greg, was just a year older than I was, and next to him lived Mitch, the oldest kid of the three houses. We were all good friends and would ring doorbells asking if the others were available "to come out and play." Before Instant Messaging over the Internet, the kids next door actually interacted face to face.

Greg's parents put up a basketball hoop above their garage when Greg no longer found pleasure in playing Ping-Pong on the table they bought him just 13 months prior.

Countless hours were spent playing "HORSE" on his hoop, though a real basketball game never surfaced, at least one that I was allowed to play in.

"You're too little, Ben. Just watch… and if the ball rolls into the street, you can go get it." This suited me fine for a while, but it left something to be desired. Oddly enough, their games stopped shortly after they had started when the next new outdoor pastime was discovered, like riding scooters, playing with remote control cars, and the ever-popular: watching TV in the garage.

The middle house seemed to be the house that was at the center of everything, but this meant it also got the most abuse. The summer heat melted water balloons onto Greg's driveway; his small lawn sported the "trampled look" regardless of what *Los Angeles Magazine* heralded as the *in* look for that season; and the landscaping never seemed to last very long. (And we discovered that gladiolas can die spontaneously during a game of HORSE.)

But as my playmates got older, they started to have less time for playing outside. Mitch was the first to no longer come out to ride bikes or play a game of catch. Then, my brother and Greg, at about the same time, found completing their homework on time to be more compelling than playing in the street past dusk.

Soon, it was just me. Sure, I had my little sister and the younger neighborhood kids, but as soon as I had made new friends with them, they seemed to move away. Actually, two families moved away within a couple months of each other, just after I had made friends with their kids. It was not a great time for playing outside.

And if trying to find a playmate to go bike riding with was not difficult enough, the neighborhood kids had found Nintendo to be the new favorite pastime. On a Saturday morning, instead of playing in front yards, in driveways, and in the street, the neighborhood kids were sitting on the rug, 12 to 18 inches from the TV screen trying to guide Link through his first adventure to Zelda or warping Mario from World 1-2 to World 4-1 or even duck-hunting with a gun full of digital bullets.

I guess it wouldn't have been so bad if I had been in the same situation as every other kid in 1989, but I had a mother who thought video games were unhealthy for children. It took my grandmother, in true grandparent style, to buy Nintendo for my brother and I without my mom knowing. It just appeared under the Christmas tree one year next to a cardboard basketball hoop and a "Build Your Own Doorbell" science kit from Santa.

Because of my mother's protection – which some might argue as over-protection – of her children's minds, playing Nintendo was a rare treat restricted to limited occurrences during summer vacation and the Christmas break. As we got older, though, my bother and I realized we could sneak the Nintendo out of the garage where it collected dust and play it while Mom was on a day-long excursion or at the store and then replace it to its dust-catching position before she returned. But while there were daylight hours and I was home, I was pushed outside.

Around the corner from our house and just across the street from the Vons Market was a used bookstore that my mom would go to every Saturday so that she could browse their new used books. I liked to go with my mom and look through the shelves for the really old books. I was amazed that they were just sitting out for anyone to touch, even the ones over 100 years old.

One Saturday, I had gone with her to see the new arrivals, and as we walked out of the store towards our car, my mom pointed out a kid from school who was rollerblading across the street in the Vons parking lot.

"You know who that is?" my mother asked me. "That's Melanie's son, Jason." I nodded.

"Jason," she yelled across the busy street. "Hello." She waved her free arm. He stopped and acknowledged her. "What are you doing? Where's your mother?"

He called back, but the rush of the cars drowned out his voice. With hand motions, he indicated that his mother was in the market. The light at the corner turned red, and the cars momentarily stopped whizzing past.

"Because my street is so busy and there are no sidewalks, I come to blade in the parking lot while she shops."

My mother looked at me and asked, "Why don't we invite him to come roller skate with you around our block. It's quieter there, and the sidewalks are good for skating. You could go around with him." I whined to her that I didn't want to (I didn't like having to meet new people, let alone play with them), but she called to him anyway: "Jason, would you like to come over and skate with Ben?"

"What?" The cars had started their roar again.

"No, mom," I whined, "I don't wanna go roller skating."

"I said," she called back slowly, annunciating each word and completely ignoring me, "Do – you – want – to – come – over – and – skate – with – Ben?"

"Oh," he yelled and then paused. "Let me ask my mom, and I'll call over to your house when we get home."

"Okay," my mother said, elated. "You have our number?" All I wanted was to get home and stop this cross-traffic exchange.

Jason nodded yet again; she waved; we got into our car; and then we were on our way home.

"He's a nice boy, Ben. It'll be good for you to get some exercise." Whenever she could, my mom would always throw that in: "get the circulation moving," "have some activity," "get out there."

"Whatever." I was angry that I had to change my plans of doing some important nothings on the final weekend of Christmas vacation. A slight nervous pain crept into my stomach.

"It'll be fun," she said again as she parked the car in the driveway.

When we got inside, I hoped Jason wouldn't call. Maybe he couldn't find the number or his mother wouldn't want him to come over. The phone rang; I crumpled up my face nervously.

"Get the phone," my mother told me.

"No, I don't want to. You get it," I said with subtle defiance.

As she went to pick up the phone, she gave me that "look" mothers make, which is more than just a facial expression. It says, "I'm disappointed in you," "Are you telling the truth," and "Come on now, do what I say" all at once.

"Hello... Oh, hi," she said. "Sure. Yeah, right now... No, no, it's no problem... Uh-huh... Yeah, come on over.... Okay... Bye." She hung up. "Lucky for you, that was his mom. She's going to drop him off. Go put on your roller skates."

I had no choice now, but the nervousness was still there; so I tried to convince myself it was excitement. He was coming over, so there was no reason why I should make it a bad experience for him, or me, for that matter. I went and put on my skates.

He arrived, already wearing his new-looking rollerblades. I was slightly embarrassed that I was using old-fashioned roller skates, which were also recently purchased, when inline skates had become the norm. We greeted each other and then just started skating down the sidewalks. We exchanged small talk; and I pointed out the "exciting parts" of the sidewalk.

"Yeah, just down here," I said, proud to share my secret cement mutation, "is where there's a huge jump because the roots have grown up under the sidewalk. It's fun to go over really fast."

"Cool." Jason raced to it just ahead of me; I moved more clumsily in my clunky skates. Jason's sleek skates carried him faster and more gracefully. He had the new BMW, and I had the 10-year-old Honda – both were reliable vehicles, but his just looked nicer and had the extra features.

We skated around my neighborhood for a while, passing the same spots over again as we circled the block. After about an hour or so, we ended up back at my garage and pulled out some bikes. Mine was a hand-me-down from James, which was a hand-me-down from our cousins. I let Jason use James's newer bike.

"Hey, that's great you have your own," he said excitedly.

"I out-grew mine, so now I have to use my mom's old one. And that's really cool... *not!*" We thought saying "not" after a sarcastic phrase was hilarious. How easily amused we were as kids.

The afternoon passed, and we laughed some more. By the time he left two hours later, our conversation was comfortable. And so goes life: when you finally feel comfortable with a situation and are starting to enjoy yourself, it's time to go. We made plans to go bike riding again soon, and I was actually looking forward to seeing the kid who had made me feel like vomiting at the thought of having to hang out with him.

In the weeks that followed, we hung out and rode bikes almost daily. Sometimes one of us was busy, but when we were both free, we would go outside and "get some activity." The growth of our friendship over the following months could have been because we lived walking distance from each other. Or, it could have been that a Thrifty's Drug Store opened across the street from his house with an ice cream counter just inside the front door, and at that time, a scoop of Chocolate Malted Crunch (the best flavor) was only 35 cents. What a way to spend a day after school: come home, change out of your uniform, call up a friend, ride bikes, get ice cream, and be home by dinner time. Life in fifth grade was good.

In the next couple of years, our pastimes changed, as did our interests; we no longer rode our bikes. It's not that we chose not to, that wasn't it at all. In fact, because of the fun we had traveling around our part of the Valley on our own, we had both purchased new bikes. And we didn't stop riding just because the apartment community near Jason's house where we most often rode our bike put up signs that read, "No trespassing, bikes, roller skates, or skate boards." Even when our parents started making us wear helmets, we got discouraged but didn't let that stop us. I think the main reason we stopped riding our bikes is that, while dropping off Jason's mom's walking shoes for long overdue repair, two guys – teenagers our own age – jumped on our unlocked bikes and stole them.

Actually, I think that was *the* reason we stopped riding.

And we weren't even inside the shop for a long time. We were actually standing at the door about to step over the threshold to get back onto our bikes when the bandits jumped on them – right there in front of us. If I hadn't frozen when I saw all my hard work that paid for the bike taken from me, I could've reached out and touched the thieves – that's how close I was.

"Ben!" Jason yelled. "Move! Go after them!"

My feet were stuck – I couldn't move. I just watched my bike as its new owner rode away on it.

"Come back!" Jason yelled pushing me out the door and then starting after the thieves.

I woke from my shock and started after them, too. We ran as fast as we could, which was not fast enough. As we turned the corner, Jason yelled to a man who was getting out of his car right near where villains were riding our bikes, "Hey, Mister, those guys stole our bikes!" The man looked up, smiled, and waved to us. A lot of help. We followed for less than a block until, out of breath and energy, we stopped and saw our bikes disappear across the street.

"Let's go back to my house. We can have my mom drive us around and find them."

I agreed as we jogged, slower after the wasted sprint, back to Jason's house. The attempt would prove fruitless, though: by the time we got back to his house, which was about a block away, I knew the bandits would be gone.

After we had finally convinced his mom we were not joking, she hurried us into her car, and we drove to look for our lost bikes.

"Which direction did they head?" she asked, seeming to be more agitated about the theft than we were.

"They cut across the street here," I said, pointing to the right. Somehow, she misunderstood and went to the left. Jason and I looked at each other confused, and then smiled.

"No, mom," he said, trying not to upset her further, "I think they went this way." He pointed the other way. She still didn't get it.

"Mom!" Jason pressed harder, "They went down this

street but turned the other way."

"Why didn't you say that?" she snapped at him, riled that our bikes had been taken, especially since it happened so close to their house. She turned the car around, but I knew it was a lost cause unless they had abandoned the bikes in the immediate area.

After about 15 minutes of unsuccessfully scouring the adjacent streets, we gave up and headed back to the house. We called the police, but they told us that unless the bikes were registered, (which they weren't) nothing could be done. So, we stopped riding bikes.

With our bikes gone and both of us getting older, our attention turned to other more important things: computer games. Because my brother was starting high school at St. Vincent's and he needed a computer for all his assignments, my parents bought one for the family. For Jason and I, this new toy was more compelling than riding bikes ever was. Jason bought games for us to play on my computer for hours on end. Before long, Jason got his own computer (to play the games, of course). We spent over a year sitting at the computer, trying to figure out games like *Heart of China, Monkey Island,* and *The Star Trek Game*.

Our passion for the computer, in turn, resurrected our interest in Nintendo. So, just before Nintendo games disappeared from the shelves of Blockbuster Video stores, we went weekly to the search for games to play. I had *The Game Genie,* which allowed for special powers in all the games, so we could beat all the games we rented before they had to be returned. All except one.

We rented the *Gilligan's Island* game four times, and even with *Game Genie,* we could never seem to beat it. One Friday night, we even played until 3 a.m., but to no avail. We tried endlessly to navigate the Skipper and Gilligan around and off the island, but the game's end was like the guys who stole our since forgotten bikes: elusive. Blockbuster stopped renting regular Nintendo games before we ever had a chance to complete that game. New video game systems continued to shove

Nintendo into video game dark ages, but none had the energy or fun that came with the original Nintendo and its games of Mario, Luigi, and Gilligan.

Now, fortunately for our friendship, Jason went to St. Vincent's two year's after James and one year before I did. Our friendship was sustained, when most of my others failed, because we remained within the same educational realm. He was able to tell me, more accurately than James, what to expect and would give me advice about how to handle different teachers. We remained friends through the years, remembering the days when we actually had bikes to ride.

Our friendship became distant, though, when I finally went to college, but I kept up my end of the friendship even through the months when he was too busy or distracted to return my calls. And it paid off, for we now see each other almost weekly. I knew that keeping up my end of the friendship could only result in a stronger relationship once he decided to call back.

And just recently, Tony, a friend of mine from stage crew at St. Vincent's, invited me to go with him and Nick to lunch.

"I can't. I've got plans to go to Jason Hamdon's for lunch. Sorry. But thanks for the invite. Next time for sure."

"Wait – you're friends with Jason Hamdon? That just blows my mind."

"Why? I have a lot of different friends?"

"I don't know, I just can't picture him hanging out with you. No offence or anything, but he was always totally making fun of people when we were in high school. I guess I figured he would have made fun of you. You know, the way a lot of those guys did."

"Nope. We've actually been friends since 5th grade."

Chiming in from the other room, Nick spoke up, "That's what's cool about you, Ben: you're always full of surprises. You're so unpredictable."

I guess I am. I wonder if growing up in the Valley will do that to a guy. Jason might tell you differently – he's known me longer than any of my friends have. But then again, he grew up in the Valley, too.

When I started driving, I learn that, sometimes, life outside of the Valley was just as interesting, if not more so. My trip that day had been proof of that, and only after an hour. But back when I started to regularly venture from Ventura Boulevard into the expanses of the rest of the city, I realized that it's all relative. Only as part of LA's family was the Valley able to thrive, just like communities of Hollywood, Westchester, Brentwood, and Eagle Rock. Los Angeles was the roots, and the branches that grew outward strengthened them.

And as I turned west onto Wilshire and headed towards the Miracle Mile, I didn't know what to expect next. But I was sure I could expect something.

NINE

Flashing warning signs and orange cones indicated that Wilshire was undergoing some road maintenance or construction of some sort – the city is always under construction. Roads are always being "improved," which actually means tearing them up for way too long before they get "fixed." It takes so long that, sometimes, when the crews are finally finished, it's almost impossible to recall what they were actually "fixing." So, when they do finally finish, the motorists presume that the "improvement" had really alleviated some traffic problems when, in reality, the only thing that had changed was that the road was finished being "improved."

The yellow caution signs were almost unnecessary as the metal plates on the road violently and repetitively heralded maintenance and all of the cars merging into a makeshift lane forced acknowledgement of the improvements. Fortunately, Sunday didn't have as much traffic as the weekdays did, so this little interruption to the flow of traffic was not as significant as it would be the next day. I could just imagine Monday morning, though, with lattes and cells and briefcases and lipstick and razors and newspapers all being punished for the traffic that resulted due to road improvement.

For the years that my parents had their rental house in Carlsbad, my dad always drove around the construction that was the 5 Freeway to get us there on weekends. From south at San Onofre (which is locally known as "The Nuclear Boobs" due to the two spherical nuclear reactors) all the way up through and past Disneyland, Cal-Trans had been working to alleviate the congestion that results from the original, limited freeway. No matter how hard and fast they work, there is always traffic due to the growth in Southern California... and those increasingly irritated Freeway Gods.

My dad knew every possible alternate route in case any stretch of freeway had traffic on it. I saw more of Southern California when I rode with my dad because his routes always included at least three freeways and any combination of surface streets, back roads, toll roads, thoroughfares, coastal cruises, mountain passes, or bridge crossings. Being able to maneuver the freeway system of Los Angeles and beyond to avoid the ever-present Sig Alerts is a fined-tuned skill that is more complex than deciphering the most challenging *New York Times* crossword puzzles.

In late May of my eighth grade year, we had one last trip scheduled to go south to the beach before my graduation. We usually picked up my brother up from St. Vincent's at noon and quickly left in order to avoid the rush hours that begin around 1:10 p.m. on Fridays. Since most of them came from 15 to 20 miles away from the centrally located Downtown LA school, St. Vincent's students were dismissed early on Fridays to avoid this same traffic condition. (I later learned while attending St. Vincent's that this early-dismissal practice was initially implemented because of the crematorium, located directly across the street, which only operated on Friday afternoons.)

That year, I was accepted at St. Vincent's (where 800 guys apply for 300 spaces), which was not that hard to fathom since my brother was a current student. But the fact that I was accepted as the "number one applicant" made my parents proud and dumbfounded me. I didn't think I was doing anything that spectacular.

I was awarded a scholarship named after a highly influential, dead priest and had to attend the school's end of the year award ceremony to be recognized. So on that day, my parents and I arrived at St. Vincent's around 11 a.m. to proudly take our place at the back corner of the auditorium in a space designated with handmade signs: "Next Year's Frosh."

Other incoming freshmen were there, too; about five of us were all receiving entrance scholarships to the prestigious college preparatory high school. I was about to be honored by entering an institution that had been graduating young men of Los Angeles for over 125 years. The rest of the auditorium was filled with seemingly rowdy freshman, sophomores, and juniors who were just about to finish another year of high school.

As I looked around the room noticing familiar faces I had encountered previously while visiting the campus, a short, jewelry-clad woman who clicked along in her extremely high heels approached my parents. She was in her mid-50s, though she tried to make herself to appear 30 years younger by the way she dressed. I know I turned red with embarrassment.

"Oh, hi," She said over-dramatically, her Spanish accent thick and exotic. "What are chu guys doing here? Have you come to *bailar*?" She had danced with my dad at the past six Parent Dances at St. Vincent's and always asked if he wanted to *baila*, even though he continually reminded her that he had taken Latin in high school, not Spanish.

My dad laughed, "Not now, Ms. de la Rosa – we're here for Ben today." He smiled at me, and then I smiled even more embarrassed. "He was accepted as the number one applicant." He beamed.

"*Ay dios mio*. Good job." She patted me on the back. "Then, I hope chu will consider taking *mi clase honores*. The Honors class. Chu will be bery good at it. Chu talk to me in *Septiembre*, okay?" Still intimidated but now flattered, I nodded.

40

"Aye, I have to sit over here with dees guys." Pointing at a group of students who were seeing who could hit the other harder, she rolled her eyes and at the same time made a face that seemed to scream, "When will all this madness end?" She smiled at us again and spouted, "*Adios*," as she clicked away as fast has she had come. If this was high school at St. Vincent's, I had no idea how I would fit in.

The mass of boys settled down as the principal came to the podium. He spoke about the end of another great year and the future; I was nervous about having to walk all the way to the front of the auditorium to receive my award.

"And to start," the principal priest continued, "we will recognize the outstanding incoming freshman."

They started calling us up one by one. The first guy received his scholarship as outstanding African-American applicant, and the second for being a Latino showing great potential. Another guy received a scholarship because of his sports' potential. The principal explained each award and then said a few words about the awardees.

"And finally, the Fr. Thomas H. Gallagher, S.J. scholarship –" with every beat of my heart, my stomach seemed to shrink, "– is given to a student who shows himself to be the top applicant to St. Vincent High School." I could feel my face turn bright red as my dad again beamed in my direction. With every word the principal spoke, my blood was pumped faster. The auditorium stretched out in front of me as he started to describe the recipients. "This year, we had two applicants who were equally superior to the rest of the applicants. The first comes from the Mayflower School in Pasadena...."

The principal went on to describe Brandon Hamurabi. He said something to the effect of he was well rounded and appeared to be very involved. To me, the tall and skinny guy looked like a caricature of a nerd with his thick glasses and awkward posture. His matted hair framed his pasty face; his apparent inability to smile made him appear very shy.

"Our second recipient," the principal continued, "Comes from the San Fernando Valley. He was student body president and shows himself to have the potential to be a great St. Vincent Lion." I was excited, now, and even more embarrassed as he flattered me as one of the newest Lions at St. Vincent's. He finished by repeating our names to a roar of applause.

We both stood, and I was the first one down the long aisle. As I nervously walked from the back of the enormous auditorium, 900 college-bound young men amusing themselves by clapping or cheering or talking or ignoring the ceremony. I vaguely saw blurs of the familiar faces of Jason and my brother and the familiar, unavoidable sparkle of Ms. De Las Rosas's jewelry.

I received my award – an envelope – and then shook the hands of the administrators on the stage. Brandon followed me back down the aisle but kept going when I awkwardly stopped and gave a high five to Ms. De Las Rosas's out-stretched hand. I had done it: no more nervousness, just sheer embarrassed excitement.

For the next four years, I relived the day we left for the beach from the ceremony. I would often remind Brandon that we both came in at number one. And when we graduated, Brandon was still number one, the valedictorian. I'm not sure what happened to me, though. Jimmy, Brandon's classmate from Mayflower, took my spot at number two in academics, and I dropped to the high teens. He wanted to vie for the number one spot, and I let him.

"You know, Jimmy," I would often tease him, "you have to remember that when we entered as freshman, I was the one that shared the top with Brandon." In the last months of school, I added, "But I am happy to relinquish to you my position, as I have taken a more talkative role in the School Rankings. You know, you can spend all day contemplating the many pros and cons about being number two in a class that exults its number one. But in my book, you're both just Mayflower students who aren't cool enough to live in the official LA." As Pasadena residents, they sometimes failed to realize the importance of being citizens of the city in which they went to school, the City of Los Angeles.

St. Vincent's left its mark on me as much as I left a mark on it, and as I drove down Wilshire headed towards the Miracle Mile, Beverly Hills, and eventually the Pacific, I recalled the days of traveling to school from the Valley. The next two miles would be like literally driving down Memory Lane, each street name carrying with it its own set of experiences.

I just had to get out of the construction zone, though, so I could keep moving along. Since I knew the area well, I also knew I could reach my destination in no time.

TEN

As I edged up to Vermont, jolted as I rolled over each metal plate laid as the substitute road, I took the opportunity to turn left and avoid Wilshire's off-road course. Out of habit and without thinking I was headed towards St. Vincent High School.

At that moment, driving down Vermont towards St. Vincent's and the 10 Freeway, it hit me: almost every day of high school I did things out of habit without realizing that they might not be normal for the average high school student. The routes that I traveled were at the top of the list. I guess the things I saw out of the window were interesting, though the hour commute that provided such views was never considered unique.

At dinner each night, I'd replay the events of the day: "Well, I saw Mr. T at a red light," I would say matter-of-factly and then paused as if I was waiting for my mom to say, "oh, and how is he doing?"

Jay Leno on Ventura Boulevard in Studio City, Julia Roberts on Highland Avenue in Hollywood, and Fabio going over Coldwater Canyon in his Hummer – all were sights reported at my dinner table. My 30-mile daily commute to high school was not all celebrities, though.

Classes didn't start until 8:15, but I had to get up almost

two hours earlier in order to get to school on time. I had to bargain the bathroom with my brother for a year; and then when he finally gave in and left for college, my sister decided to fight me for the precious moments before my carpool would honk me out of the house.

See, until I got my license, I had to depend on the generosity of upperclassmen to get a ride to and from school or else I had to take the even longer bus ride. Fortunately, I had a regular carpool that would drive me, so I only had to take the unnecessarily long bus ride a few times.

For my freshman year, Mark, who lived just below Mulholland Drive on the Valley side, shuttled my brother and I through LA. James tried to get his license when he turned sixteen but failed. He went out to the Glendale DMV (where it was supposedly easier than the Van Nuys branch), but he said a tall orange cone which was marking the space he had to park within was "blown by the Santa Anas" into the car. He was scarred by the experience and didn't get his license until the year after he returned from college, which was not in LA.

Mark drove a Jeep Cherokee and, everyday without fail, would play his mix tape with "Blister in the Sun" on it. His car reeked of the Chin-Chin salad dressing that had spilled on our way home from lunch one of the first Fridays of the school year. I always sat behind my brother and worked on homework as the two of them would enjoy the freedom of driving, James vicariously.

The first half of the drive took us on the 101 Southbound through the Cahuenga Pass. Usually, just as we would pass Universal Studios and emerge into Hollywood, the freeway would come to a complete stop. There was never an accident or a huge influx of cars at the Highland onramp; we just left our house at the right time so that when we reached the other side of the aforementioned Pass, the sun was shining directly into all the drivers' eyes. And if the sun didn't blind you, the red brake lights would. The God of the 101 reveled at the natural advantage he had in keeping motorists on His freeway.

"Just wait until 7:15," my mom offered when my brother

first explained the solar phenomenon. In theory, hers was a good idea except that the regular, non-blinded traffic can delay the normally 20-minute drive to up to 45 minutes if we didn't leave at 7 a.m. The longer we waited before we left, the more crowded the essential surface streets that made up the larger portion of the commute were.

So, the blaring sun forced us off the freeway at Vine Street to cut through Hollywood toward the heart of LA. Sure, on lucky days the freeway was clear all the way to Vermont Avenue, but the MTA – for as long as I could remember and beyond my last day of high school – had Vermont under construction, trying to install a traffic-reducing subway system into The City of Freeways. Unforeseen delays could occur at any moment and bring traffic to a ten-minute dead stop – and the Freeway Gods celebrate.

Ninety percent of the time, though, no matter what time we left, the last leg of the commute usually commenced with a trip down Vine Street. Passing the Capitol Records Building, we would travel from glittering Hollywood (with homeless sleeping in doorways along the Walk of Fame) to the elite neighborhoods of Hancock Park, which I regard as one of the first suburbs of Los Angeles, which is now in the heart of the vast city. Tree-canopied streets, the Wilshire Country Club, and Larchmont Boulevard – the one-block, commercial main street for the five-square mile neighborhood (and those who wished they could live there) - define the community of homes modestly comparable to those of Beverly Hills. But this pocket of wealth and prosperity is quite limited.

The areas just outside of Hancock Park's boundaries were more destitute the closer that I got to school, and I fondly referred to the area between Hancock Park and St. Vincent's as "The Land of a Thousand Couches." No matter what day of week or time of day, couches were always strewn about on the side of the road. Main streets like Western and Pico, small streets like Barendo or 12th, and especially alleys – all were home to couches. Occasionally, a TV might also be cooling off on the sidewalk near the couch. And on a lucky day, a coffee table or barstool would be sunning along Normandie, accenting the grazing couches. With this abundance of outdoor seating, I've always wondered what was in the living rooms of these residences.

Arriving at school, a sense of comfort would set in. A police escort was needed to walk along the streets just two blocks from my high school's campus, but once within a block of the school, everything was at ease. The cemetery across the street was calming; the monstrous city buses that stopped near the school's entrance hummed a familiar tune; the bark of the seemingly rabid stray dogs that roamed through the neighborhood still scared the crap out of me.

In my sophomore year, my brother and Mark had graduated, and I was lucky enough to be able to catch a ride to school with Jason. He didn't like the 101 route; he instead preferred the "over Coldwater Canyon" pattern. As we sped through the curves that took us to the top of the Hollywood Hills and then back down through the estates of Beverly Hills, I felt a connection to the city. These were the same roads Lucy and Desi traveled as they passed through Beverly Hills to get to The RKO Studios, the same roads that poured young lovers from the top of Mulholland Drive into the abyss of the elite.

We picked up Paul, another sophomore, in Beverly Hills and then headed down La Cienega towards Venice Boulevard. As we approached St. Vincent's from the west, the couches were not as abundant, but I felt the same emotions as we passed from Beverly Hills into the neighborhoods that brought to LA "Norma's Unisex Barber and 98 Cent Store." But in my second year at St. Vincent's, the real anomalies ran through the streets as we drove through Beverly Hills.

Eventually, with the money I had saved since I started working for my dad at five-years-old, I bought my own car, a 1987 BMW 325, my freedom. I drove to school and even had my own carpool. Sometimes, there was no traffic; sometimes we would be delayed up to an hour. No matter the route, the drive was always uniquely LA. My car was my key to the city, and by that time, I was ready to unlock any of its doors.

"How did you drive those freeways everyday?" my college friends from up north would question when they heard of my educational commute. "LA has such terrible driving conditions – and the drivers are horrible."

"No," I would reply, "LA has great drivers. It's just that, compared to the rest of you, we move at the speed of life. Angelenos don't mosey through country roads to get to the grocer. We move to where we are going, and we move fast."

Even without power steering, I had the power to steer my future, to choose which route to take to school, to navigate Los Angeles. I learned about LA on the way to school; I studied LA on the way home. I had school five days a week, 36 weeks a year, for four years: over 21,000 miles of education. My parents had to pay for me to go to St. Vincent's, but the drive there was free.

ELEVEN

The drive down Vermont was the longest stretch of straightaway I had driven that day, and it gave me a chance just to sit and drive and think. I tried to avoid thinking about my ridiculous cell phone, which was almost all I could think about. I would've much rather just driven aimlessly, exploring, than having to get somewhere specific.

Driving without a destination had been one of my favorite things to do since I first got my car. Sometimes, I would just drive down a street until I couldn't take it any more. My favorite route was to drive from Ventura Boulevard until it turns into Cahuenga, which spills into Highland, which then melts into La Brea, which twists into Hawthorne, which travels through Palos Verdes and then becomes Pacific Coast Highway all the way down to San Clemente. That powerful drive is the most thoughtfully indirect way to from LA to San Diego in about four hours.

But as I sat on Vermont with signs in various Romantic, Germanic, Asiatic, and even Bantu languages surrounding me, I couldn't help but notice how different this neighborhood was from my own; yet, I still felt like I was part of it. I've always taken pride in being from Los Angeles, both the stereotypically good and not-so-good parts. Sections of Vermont Avenue were home to some of the not-so-good parts, by reputation. But being immersed in the area, driving through the side streets into the neighborhoods, trying to understand what defined this community – through these actions, I was linked to this area as much as my own Valley community and, in turn, all of LA.

One sign in particular stands out in my memory, a quintessential LA sign: "Welcome New Yorkers," is read with "*bienvenidos*" written below it. Apparently, the expectation that New Yorkers would be stopping at this newsstand versus all the others that sold lottery tickets and bus passes required such a sign. I wondered if I was welcome there – not because I didn't speak Spanish, but because I was not from New York. Why would someone want to alienate their own city?

But Vermont has more than just multilingual signs; Vermont has signs of the times. Vermont – along with Crenshaw, Jefferson, and any number of others – was a street ablaze in the 1992 "uprisings." Over ten years ago, LA saw some of its worst devastation, and it wasn't from an earthquake – that came two years later.

Living in the Valley, I saw the TV coverage and the Hummers rolling down Sepulveda Boulevard. I wasn't really scared, but I was nervous because I realized that this wasn't news from another country and the Hummers weren't the ones owned by celebrities and show-offs.

My future high school was built in the center of the city (just off Vermont) at the start of the 20th century and remained where it was built, even after it was in the center of that year's media-fed chaos. My brother James was a freshman at St. Vincent's that April, and for three days, the school was closed because of the turmoil surrounding the gates of the school. Some cities have "snow days"; in 1992, LA had "unrest days".

At dinner the night of his first day back at school in May, James told of the drive to and around school: burnt out buildings, trash, and people everywhere. I was enthralled that such a thing, the things that ignited the pages of my history book, was happening in my lifetime. I would never forget the experience that was national, history-making news within my own city.

Three years later, when I got to St. Vincent's, I made friends with guys who lived throughout Los Angeles. I was not thinking about the destruction, havoc, and ignorance that were wrought upon the city for three days that spring; I was more focused on making new friends in a brand new school that was located in a struggling area of LA. It was apparent that the unrest of '92 had occurred in the area, but it was no longer as interesting as the news promoted it to be.

Not until my junior year did the events of five years prior once again take hold of the news. Every local and some national news shows were doing updates on "South Central " "five years after the fires," almost intentionally ignoring the fact that the "uprisings" occurred all over the city, not just in the mythical land of "South Central" (a place that seems to be the location of every incident happening outside of the Valley or the coastal communities). And, with TV being such a large part of my daily routine, I was obligated to bring it up the next day at school.

Five years and one day after the start of the second major civil unrest of Los Angeles in the second half of the 20th century, I was eating lunch and talking with Ryan and Marco. "Can you believe it's been five years? It seems like just yesterday." I was always the one to start conversations... or steer them.

"It really does seem like yesterday. Too close." Ryan seemed to be lost in a gaze while eating his apple.

"Yeah, that was a crazy time down here. You wouldn't believe the shit I saw happen in my neighborhood. " Marco lived just a few miles from school. I'd been to his house a couple of times when I'd given him a ride home, and his neighborhood looked like an urban, distant cousin of mine: family dwellings with yards and pets. But the houses there were older, Victorian-looking homes built, perhaps, at the same time as the beautiful homes of Hancock Park, but unkempt and decrepit. Slumlords existed, and they used the homes of early, modern LA with their incredible architecture as a means of repressing the poor. Even worse was that, if you went just three blocks out onto the main avenues, the neighborhood swarmed with aggressiveness.

"I'm sure," I said, intrigued by someone who experienced it first hand, not filtered through the blades of news helicopters. "How close were you to the action? I mean, did you know anyone who was affected by it?"

"We were all affected by it. You, me, Marco – everyone," Ryan said sharply.

"Oh, I know. I just felt like someone who was in the heat of the happenings might have a story about it or something."

"Yeah," chimed in Marco, "I think my experience of looters and fires holds more interest, I guess, than Ben's story about fearful Valley residents."

Ryan responded seriously, his inflections revealing the effect of his experience. "I know. It's just that my family was really affected by it." He paused naturally, further peeking my interest. "My parents had this store near our house, which is not too far away from here, and we lost almost everything during the riots. On the last day of the riots, we thought we had come through without losing our store. The stores next to us, behind us, across the street, everywhere – they were all vandalized or burnt. My parents had been fair about the way they treated the customers; we thought they had spared us." He shook his head.

"Whoa, I never knew that. What happened?" I was intrigued at the first-hand account. Marco listened in silence.

"So it was the last night, the Saturday. My parents and uncles had been out there almost the whole time watching the store but also making sure that they weren't too obvious. They kept an eye on the store, protecting it from the local herds. One of the things that helped keep it safe was the fact that it was situated next to a two-story building with an office and a Beauty parlor – which no one had any interest in – and a cleaners that had been shut down and boarded up for a while."

"Jeez, that's amazing."

"Yeah...I guess. But from the TV at home, I saw that everything was being burnt: libraries, churches, markets – everything. My parents told me to stay inside and watch my brother and cousins, but when they had both left to go help a neighbor, I snuck out and ran a few blocks up the street to see what was happening. I saw my uncles sort of hanging out on a corner, and I stayed near them. It was about eight o'clock and the smoke filled the air and our lungs. I felt dirty with the visibly floating ash.

"People were everywhere, I remember. I don't remember faces or anything, but both adults and kids were out in the streets. Just outside. Like me. And it wasn't just black people like the news put it on TV."

"So, what happened with your parents when they came back and you weren't there? I'm sure they were worried."

"Well, my dad had come out to my uncles and when he saw I was there, he was angry for an instant, but he told me to go home before my mother got frightened. He told me nothing was going to happen and that he had heard from the TV that it would all be over soon. So, I ran home to my mother. She was practically hysterical when I got home; I heard her swearing in Korean with words that I didn't even know. I thought I was gonna get it, but when I went inside, she ran to me and hugged me so tight I could barely breath. She held me for a long time, too. I was like, 'Why are you hugging me so long?' I guess she had found out that the neighbors had lost their son during the riots, and my mom was scared."

"I know how that is. After the earthquake, my mom wouldn't let me go anywhere without worrying that I was going to get crushed by a falling building or freeway. What about you, Marco? Was your mom that way?"

"Yeah, I guess."

"You guess?" I turned back to Ryan. "So what ended up happening?" Sometimes my steering was a little erratic, but I had to get the conversation back on track.

"Well, I went to bed that night encouraged. The next morning, my mom woke me up early. Her eyes were swollen with tears. I thought for sure someone else had died. Then she told me that the store was gone. Apparently in the middle of the night, a mixed crowd – a mob of sorts – was roaming the streets as a herd and came across the store untouched and approached with one of those Molotov cocktails. I guess my relatives tried to stop them, but then the group started hurling rocks. My father kept saying from the start of the riots that these things were not worth getting injured or killed over. They tried to talk the crowd out of it but failed to make them see reason. No police were around, so my father had to step aside and let the pack have their way. He stood by and watched as they threw the bottle through the window. I guess there was not much that could be done.

"One of my older cousins had run to call the police and upon his return was immediately sent back to call the fire department. They didn't get there until the store was almost gone.

"That Sunday we spent the day sifting through the store, for anything salvageable. Not much was left. My hands were black with muddy ash. It was exactly what I thought would happen but was told wouldn't."

"Man. That's terrible. But you were able to rebuild, right? I mean you guys have a store now?" I knew they still had a store because I had driven him there, too.

"Yeah, my parents were able to use their savings to start again over in the Fairfax District. It's not the same though. They're still struggling to overcome that one night. The TV doesn't tell you that part in their retrospectives."

"Yeah. That's true." Marco agreed.

In an attempt to realize a connection of experience, I think I then told them part of my Northridge Earthquake story, but nature's destruction of a building or business doesn't really have quite the same effect as destruction by a force of citizens. Ryan finished his lunch and went off to a meeting; I was left sitting momentarily silent with Marco.

"That's an incredible story… I had no idea." Truly flabbergasted, I groped for words: "I bet a lot of people have stories from those three days that put my 'Valley fears,' as you call them, to shame."

"Yeah, I guess." Marco had been especially quiet.

"What's with you? Doesn't this stuff affect you at all?"

"Sure it does. But different."

"Oh. How's that? Something different happen in your neighborhood?"

"Same sort of thing. I don't live too far from Ryan, you know – just a little farther up Vermont. Same sorta stuff happened in my neighborhood. It's just different, though."

"How?" I continued to question – he had my interest sparked by his take on the whole experience. "How was it different – were you one of the looters or something?" I joked.

He didn't say anything for a second, then, shot me with an uncomfortable arrow. "Not exactly."

"What?" I paused, again in disbelief. "No way. You're joking, right?"

"Well, I didn't do anything everyone else wasn't doing. You can't say anything to anyone, okay? I feel awful now, but at the time, I was caught up in the craziness of it all. Man, it was so crazy out there, you don't even know. We barely slept for the days it was happening – half out of fear and half out of excitement. Man, you can't say anything, though."

"I won't. I won't. But, jeez, what did you do? I mean, what did you take?"

"Shit, I'm not thief – I wasn't looting or anything." He became defensive. "I was just running around with my friends and all the older kids of the neighborhood. We just ran around and went wild. It was… just… crazy. I can't really explain. Looking back, I feel so guilty. I haven't told many people, but everyone from this area knows because everyone from this area did it."

"Jeez, that's quite an experience." I couldn't believe what I was hearing.

"Yeah, I guess. Ya know, though, the weird thing is that, at the time, it felt great. Finally, the power was in our hands. That's what my older cousin kept saying, and it made sense, too. I saw the stores I bought candy in go up in flames, and it felt good... sort of. I wasn't angry or anything, I was just in control."

"You should write a story about that – it's really interesting."

"Yeah, I really don't like to talk about it, though. You promise you're not going to say anything to anyone, right?"

"Yeah, no way. I'm just lucky you told me – I would have never known." I would have never expected Marco, a sharp, honor student who enjoyed *Star Trek,* to be a part of the destruction of his own neighborhood. I guess it's hard for some to stand up against a larger, influential group.

I was intrigued at what I had heard five years after the fact, though. Every time I drove down Vermont, I couldn't help but think of the incidents that shaped my perception of humanity in the city. Ryan being devastated by the riots and Marco being a participant in that devastation led me to realize the complexities of LA's citizenry. I didn't press Ryan further on the topic because I saw how much emotion was connected to it. And only once more did I bring the topic up to Marco.

Towards the end of senior year as I drove him back to his house, I asked Marco to point out places on Vermont that he had encountered during those three days of civil unrest. He pointed at locations where rebuilt fast food stores were, a super market, and some small stores that lined the street.

"And remember how Ryan said his parents had owned a store over here in this area? Well, that parking lot there is where it used to be."

"How do you know where it was? Did you used to go in there?"

"No." He looked out the window.

"Well, how did you know, then?"

Without looking back at me, he responded frankly, "I was there the night it was burnt down."

I felt like I knew too much already, so I didn't ask anything else. I would have loved to pick his brain, and Ryan's, too, but I knew enough without having to ask. His comment made me think why: Why certain friendships? Why live in LA? Why keep going?

I had two friends from the same neighborhood who were also friends with each other, yet one was part of the pain of the other. Why?

Vermont has a lot of dips in the road – paving them over prolongs the street's life for a while, but every time it rains, these potholes resurface under the burnt rubber of the speeding cars' tires.

TWELVE

As I headed south past Pico, sirens brought me back to the reality of Vermont. I slowed down and pull over to the right, whereas the car in front of me just sped up. Some people never move over to the right unless they themselves are the ones being pulled over. I waited for an ambulance or a police car to whiz by - that would have been too simple, though.

As the sirens grew louder, I saw an undercover cop car with just one tiny siren obnoxiously screaming its approach. After it routinely whirled past the stopped traffic, I attempted to merge back into my lane; but wouldn't you know, before I had a chance to pull back out and continue on my way, I was halted by another speeding vehicle. Right behind the undercover cop was a typical LA news van speeding – predatorily chasing – a live, breaking, on-the-scene news story.

Local news in LA shapes the way the city is viewed, deciding what's important to report and what's not. This local news defines the city to the world, and the news directors, the unseen decision-makers behind the camera, create the city, shaping and molding it into something that may or may not exist. I always think about the time NBC4 followed a story about a pigeon stuck in the studio's rafters.

LA's news has taken a whole new approach to reporting what's happening, too. Live and on the spot isn't good enough anymore. Now, it has to be all over the place at once and in 3-D with a free-gift if you watch now while they're doing the seventeenth traffic report! And that format is boring compared to the people reporting and anchoring the news.

The field reporters are as over-dramatic as some of the city's worst waiters. Using an artistic shot, a reporter will stand on freeway overpasses or behind school fences as they narrate the scene of a freeway fiasco or a detention debacle. Their voice-overs have the power of a Baptist preacher as they recount the tale of a late night hit and run accident involving "a 17-year-old male in full costume and make-up coming home of an evening of drama and artistic expression." These were not the hard-hitting reporters that the *LA Times* retained for riot coverage and investigative reports on incompetent shuttle bus drivers.

Sharing limelight with other minor stars that make up the scene of "Hollywood-in-LA," the news anchors are the real stars. Seemingly out of touch with reality, these men and women convey the news as a somber as they can force a frown or as light as they can fake it. And it seems to pay off.

And on top of that, our anchors are traded like baseball players, except they are all free agents with contacts that are broken all the time. A station will lure an anchor to their side one week with the release of their current anchor who will then go to a rival station to host a morning show while having the option to fill in for the 11 o'clock news. Like balls in a pinball machine, they bounce back and forth seeking the "sweeter deal."

But don't get me wrong – I'm not complaining. I've seen local news in other cities, and though LA's may be a little more "Hollywood," they are much more professional than most of the nation's. It's always comforting to know you can count on Fritz for weather or Fred for sports or Sam for entertainment news and Beverly for an on the scene report that really makes you think. Let's just hope the national news doesn't get a glimpse and steal them away like they did with Tom Brokaw.

And, of course, I'm speaking from a professional point of view as a newsman. Well, as a former newsman. My experience goes beyond my sixth grade field trip to *The Los Angeles Times*. Seeing the presses unroll, print, cut, and fold the over-a-century-old rag was just like watching the episode of *Sesame Street* in which they portrayed the manufacturing of crayons. We saw the administrative offices, the layout boards, and how the staff – artists, editors, writers, secretaries, bosses, runners – scurried around their work ignoring the touring class. The creation and distribution of the printed word intrigued me from that early age, and so, when each student received one of those long reporter's pads and a *Los Angeles Times* pencil – my most vivid memory of the trip – my interest was confirmed.

Three years later, while still holding onto the visions of automated folding machines and the smell of the overworked presses, I got involved with my high school's newspaper, *The Centurion*. Our newspaper was different from the *Times*, though: it was a quarterly high school publication in magazine format that was distributed late every issue. But other than that, it was almost identical. It attracted me, a young freshman, because it was a "real" publication, not just a Xeroxed copy that my grammar school called a newspaper. I was impressed.

Most high school clubs give freshman the "oh, thanks for joining – when you're a junior or senior, you might actually be able to do something; but for now, just do all the grunt work." Intimidated and apprehensive, I was only able to walk into the paper's meeting because so many other newcomers were joining at the same time. And my friend Doug, the only other guy who went St. Vincent's with me from our grammar school, encouraged me to do it by saying he would, too. That was reason enough for me – I knew initially I wouldn't be completely alone.

During the third week of school, the first newspaper meeting was held during lunch in the moderator's classroom. I walked into the packed room and imagined that, if you added girls and alcohol, this must be what a cocktail party was like. Guys were standing around eating their lunches, mingling with each from conversation to conversation, laughing too loudly at jokes that were not funny – I knew no one.

I sat in a desk at the front of the room, which was not nearly as crowded as the back of the room and the area around the teacher's desk. I saved the desk next to me for Doug, putting my backpack on it to create the illusion of occupation. Once the meeting started, I moved my bag, yet the seat sat empty for the rest of the meeting. And only afterward did I find out that Doug did in fact show up but had to stand in the back because he didn't realize I had saved him a seat. Without Doug, familiarity, I anxiously and impatiently awaited the start of the "informational meeting."

The teacher finally strolled in, his hair completely white like Christopher Lloyd's "Doc Brown" and his entourage in tow. He was the sophomore English teacher for the non-honors classes, and he was ten minutes late to the meeting. I wasn't sure what I had gotten myself into.

He continued to have his loud, private conversations with his followers for a few more minutes before he acknowledged the 40 other students in his room. He ruled this land, and these experienced "newspaper-men" were his subjects. I watched him intently, studying the way he interacted with the senior editors before the start of the meeting, but he never looked back.

He waved his followers off as he walked toward the center of the room in an effort to begin the meeting. Just before he called for the entire group's attention, he looked down at me.

"*Monsieur* Grenaro," he said in a French accent, "welcome."

Shock. He knew my name... he knew who I was... he thought I was French.

His raspy voice accentuated his sharp, white hair. His character developed just by his speaking and introducing the newspaper and the production process. The character of Mr. Jackie is embedded in the mind of everyone with whom he interacted. His personal antics as a child of the sixties, he later told us, added to his eccentricity. A student who paid attention could realize that Mr. Jackie was a recovering hippie for whom everyday was a challenge.

He knew who I was, though, and that was what impacted me. I was instantly encouraged and excited to be a part of this endeavor. Now, my mind joined the race with my heart as the meeting got going: how did he know me, I wondered in between ideas of how I could make this newspaper mine by the time I was a senior like the those to whom Mr. Jackie had turned over the meeting by that point. I was going to repay him for knowing me. I was ready and on my way.

The meeting ended, and still on my recognition-high, I signed up to write a section for the Campus News Department. I was excited that I was going to be affiliated with an organization – a club – that was, in my mind, very welcoming.

As I was walking out of the door, Mr. Jackie had sat back at his desk and was shuffling some papers in a way that looked like he was just doing that: just shuffling - not actually doing any real work or organizing. I turned back, and after two others had finished flattering him, I approached his cluttered desk.

"Mr. Jackie?" I said timidly.

"Oh, hey Mr. Grenaro." He replied jovially, like we had known each other for years and were old pals.

"Um, how do you know who I am? I'm just a freshman."

"You're James Grenaro's brother – I always told him your name sounded great in French. By the way, thanks for being here. It's great to have interested freshman around."

"No problem. See you later." I said uncomfortably and still somewhat confused.

I left anticipating a great experience working with *The Centurion*. I thought I would fit in fairly well at the newspaper/magazine. I later found out from Jason, who had Mr. Jackie during the period after lunch, that the eccentric journalism moderator told his class how impressed he was with the freshmen who were so ambitious this year. Always make the effort, and the rewards will come.

That first year, I wrote for every issue of the *Centurion*, even thought they were just small items. The next year, though, Mr. Jackie resigned from the moderator position, letting one of his former students who had since graduated from LMU with an English degree take over his position as moderator. With Mr. Jackie's departure, I too left the periodical to pursue other interests, though I never abandoned the idea of working with the magazine.

I got a job my sophomore year, trying to get some real work experience after working at my parent's store for all those years. After a year working at different retail stores, for family friends, and even babysitting for a family in the hills above Studio City, it was time to return home: I started working for my dad again and got back involved with activities at school.

I was drawn back to the publication more heavily, acting as Assistant Campus News Editor in my junior year where I started writing larger articles. And then, in my senior year, was selected to be the magazine's Business Manager. So, while I sold a record number of ads, I also wrote a feature article for each issue. My last article: a business review on student jobs and making money.

Somewhere along the line, I realized that if I wasn't going to be in the news, I better be a part of it somehow. Maybe someday, I'll be able to shape the image of LA by reporting its status. Then again, I'm no news anchor or on-the-scene, late-breaking news reporter.

THIRTEEN

Pulling back onto the road, I realized I was about to pass my old high school. I hadn't seen a school newspaper from there in a while; and though it was a Sunday during summer and I was on a mission to get that phone taken care of, I still slowed down to see if there was one in the rack. I should've known that there wouldn't be one there, but I still crawled past the front of the school that helped me mature.

I coasted along, trying not to stop traffic but still able to take a good look at my old campus to see if any changes had been made since I was there last. No new statues, walkways, or parking lots were apparent this time.

The security guard, stolid and looking like a retired wrestler, sat - as he always did - on his stool and glared at the passing motorist and occasional, out of place pedestrians. He was not like bank security: 200 years old and sitting in a chair in the corner. No, Jerry was probably 200 pounds and had defended the school during the riots. School lore has him with his gun drawn telling passersby to keep moving. He was friendly to the students, though, always giving us a nod or a movement of his hand that wasn't anything close to a wave but was definitely not just a twitch.

We had security guards not to keep the students in line, but to keep the neighborhood out. The neighborhood was once a great in its heyday… 70 years ago. But as the years passed, the neighborhood declined. During the 60s, the school had toyed with the idea of moving into a nicer area. But it was decided that St. Vincent High School stay where it was so that it could continue to serve the neighborhood by maintaining the area's level of safety because of its presence. This indirect service to the immediate communities of Pico-Union and Mid-City elevated the area to a point that could never have been achieved if it were just another commercial or residential property in a poor neighborhood. And direct service was making a mark, too, thanks to the students.

As an all-boys Catholic college prep high school, St. Vincent's required its students to do community service each semester. Some guys put it off, delaying graduation, and others got it done well in advance. I was neither an underachiever nor an overachiever – I was a guy who fell in the middle category of getting it done, but just in the nick of time.

I really did enjoy doing the community service, and it meant more because I knew it was a way I could make a small difference for someone else. I always say, why be alive if you can't make the world a better place by your existence. It's a butchery of some famous person's quote, I'm sure, but it works for me.

See, with everything that is great about LA comes some things that could use a little help. (And by "a little," most of the time, it means "a lot.") I learned this from going to St. Vincent's.

Located in the Byzantine-Latino Corridor, Pico Heights, Harvard Heights – it's all the same – St. Vincent's was in the best area to help a community in need. I'm convinced that St. Vincent's presence prevented the surrounding blocks from falling into complete degeneration, considering the outskirts of the neighborhood were not even safe for residents. The local homes, beautifully built Victorians, had grayed with age and neglect by the owners, and the renters – the residents – could barely afford to live in them. The community had such potential, and I wanted to help it out.

Outside of the required community service, which could be done anywhere in Greater LA, I was also a part of St. Vincent's volunteer Service Club (not the one that volunteered at football games or school events) that assisted the community immediate to the school and as a whole. I loved to go to the planning meetings where the whole group, all seven of us, would discuss activities that high schoolers could do and would enjoy. Most of my ideas were not things you would normally see, but all were proposed with sincerity and the community in mind.

You can probably recite, verbatim, the cries of service organizations, as most people can: "feed the hungry," "clothe the homeless," "clean the beach," "give money for the poor," "save the whales." All are noble and worthwhile causes, but I figured - and still believe - that young people need more than just a cry of "help someone less fortunate that you." If you want to get young people involved, a twist is needed – and I had some ideas.

The first thing I suggested was to change the "Christmas Clothes Drive," from what had been a lame excuse of a clothes collection, into a real clothes gathering experience.

"We need to have a catchy slogan if we want it to work," I said. "What about 'Naked Clothes Drive?'"

"Um, Ben. No," Mr. Funghe, the moderator, laughed at me. "We're trying to get people to give us clothes for the homeless, not scare them away."

"Fine. What ideas do you guys have?" I turned to the other seven members of the group. Most stared back blankly as if they were thinking. Then Neal, the club's president, responded:

"I dunno. I sorta like the 'naked' idea. It's real catchy." He laughed.

"Oh, God – not you, too." Mr. Funghe had a good sense of humor and would never get upset or reject our ideas; he would just try to get us to think of better ones. This was his last year at St. Vincent's because the following summer, he would be going to Berkeley to finish his religious studies before being ordained a full-fledged Jesuit priest.

"Okay. I got it, then! What about the 'Shirt-Off-Your-Back Clothes Drive?'" I really liked this slogan, even better than the naked one.

"That's not bad, but I liked the 'naked' one better," fake-whined Neal. "What about *nude,* instead?"

"No slogans with 'naked' *or* 'nude' in it! Got it?" Mr. Funghe chuckled in frustration, which made me laugh because I knew he was annoyed but wanted to laugh.

"Fine," I said. "We'll keep our clothes on. Let's do the 'shirt-off-the-back' thing; it's catchy. It'll make people remember to bring clothes."

And it did. We settled on that, and the clothes drive was huge success. No one really gave the clothes they were wearing, but they would go home and bring in last season's Gap or an unworn, Hawaiian shirt knockoff, forced to the back of the closet because it was not cool enough to wear.

We created other events too, all with the idea of keeping them exciting in mind. For Human Rights Awareness Week, which normally just entails a speaker coming and talking to anyone interested (usually no one), we opened an "Awareness

Café" where, in the main quad during lunch, we had the three most notorious teachers "serve" Tommy's burgers to an essay contest winner and nine of his guests. For a food drive for the homeless, I invented a new day of the week: Orange Tuesday. For the entire month of February, we reminded the school that every Tuesday was Orange Tuesday. They brought oranges that we could then pass out to hungry homeless people. This was the most effective fresh fruit because it didn't need to be washed, and we could collect oranges in big crates without damaging the actual fruit. That was fairly successful, too.

But the event that made the most impact on me and on the community was a cleanup we coordinated in conjunction with Earth Day. A community clean-up has been done, you might think. But it was more that just walking out of the school gates and picking up trash – it was a production. We wanted to show that just an hour after school could make a difference.

We started to plan this community cleanup at the end of February to occur in March. First, we set goals: clean up both sides of the streets that formed the perimeter around the school and the neighboring local church that served the poor community. The designated area was the perimeter of six city blocks - easily accomplished after school one day with a group of students.

So, we set our date, and then Mr. Funghe offered some assistance at the next meeting.

"Okay guys, I did some checking, and I think that with what we are trying to do, we need to make sure it's okay with the city. So, I called over to Bureau of Streets Services, and they are thrilled with the idea, but they had two suggestions. First, they want to send one of their people to assist us. Not coordinate or tell us what to do, but to be there for expertise."

Neal, in true form, immediately questioned this: "What kind of expertise does it take to determine whether a scrap of paper or can on the ground is trash or not?"

"I don't know, but why would we turn down help? That expert is going to be bringing supplies for you to use, so I wouldn't complain about it." That shut him up momentarily;

we hadn't even thought about how we were going to get the supplies to clean the area.

"The second thing they suggested was that we alert the LAPD so that they are aware of what's happening. They even suggested that, because of the area we were attempting to work in, the police escort us as we walk through the neighborhood."

We started delegating responsibilities for what was growing from a neighborhood cleanup to a one-day community revitalization project. But we needed to get volunteers to make the project work.

At first, there wasn't very much interest; but after we started walking around at lunch with trash bags and signs that said, "Cleanup means more than trash," guys started wondering what we were about. We carried clipboards with sign-up slips and flyers for the event. And because it was after school, we even suggested that people tell their friends and family, if they wanted.

The idea of having it right after school on a Thursday was in hopes that we would get visibility in the community by passersby and also be able to have the support of more of the student body. Most guys could easily give an hour after school, and when we started advertising the "thank you" barbeque, that sealed the deal. Guys were signing up their friends and people were truly becoming interested.

What happened next, I couldn't have imagined. Derek, a fellow senior from Redondo Beach, had heard what we were trying to do, and he walked up to me after our math class and practically floored me.

"I heard you're trying to clean up the area around school in a few weeks."

Always the salesman, I started selling him on the idea: "yeah, we are going to try to get a huge group to move through the surrounding streets and really clean it up. You've signed up, right?"

"Well, I can't. I work at this nursery over in the South Bay after school. But, I was wondering if you could use some small plants if I got them donated. You know, to plant around for beautification - you think you could use them?"

I didn't know if we could use them; I didn't even know if we could keep them alive long enough to even try to plant them - but I was never one to turn down a donation. I told him to find out exactly what he could get and I would find out how they could be used. We stayed in touch as I again contacted the Bureau of Street Services. They said that plants had to be approved by fitting a standard description and planted by the group. We made sure they were.

So, Derek's little plants turned into two-foot pots of various, locally indigenous foliage. This was no small donation, either; he got us 20 plants and the fertilizer, too.

While I was working with plants, Neal had gotten a donation of paint from one of his Culver City friends. This would be used to cover a few heavily graffiti-ed walls adjacent to the school.

Some of the other Service Club members had designed a T-shirt to be printed for the day of the event. At first, the shirts were just going to be for the coordinators, but the company gave us such a great price break that with some money allocated to us in the school budget for clubs, we were able to buy shirts for the first 50 people to sign up, and after that t-shirts would only cost $2.50, our cost.

Plants, paint, and printed shirts – the day was turning out perfectly.

When the day finally arrived, we had signed up over 60 volunteers. The support from the administration was surprisingly large: they went so far as to ask that teachers make a point to discuss the event in their classes, if it fit into their lesson. (At a Catholic school, that "if" meant "make.") We even had teachers sign up to help. The reaction was overwhelming.

On the designated Thursday, we made our move. Neal and I excused ourselves from our last period to prep the staging area. Everyone met in front of the school – a total of over 75 students, parents, teachers, and priests – where we had set up all the tools and created action plans for the spaces where we were going to be working. One group walked across the street to paint graffiti, one to the planting areas, and two around an eight-block perimeter to clean up as part of the originally intended trash patrol. Within about an hour, the wall was painted, the trash was gone, and new landscaping was completed on a traffic median next to the school courtesy of Derek, who had taken the day off to lead the planting. All this was done, of course, with a full police escort.

The Senior Officer who coordinated the escort said that she had never seen any group come together and do so many things in one day with such a small group of coordinators. Now, maybe she didn't see too many cleanups or maybe she was just trying to be encouraging, but she made us feel like we had changed the world forever.

By 5 p.m., we had everyone back to the main grass area on campus for a "thank-you," Dodger-dog barbeque of donated meats. Even the city employees were able to stay and share in our success; we were a sea of green shirts and wide grins.

What was really impressive and made it all worthwhile wasn't the aesthetic beauty, which lasted longer than we even expected: about a month. Unfortunately, the trash clandestinely blew back onto the streets, graffiti "appeared," and only about five of the plants lived through the end of the school year. What we had done to brighten the surface of the neighborhood was nice, but what really made an impact on me was what happened after just about everyone had left.

As Neal and I were packing up and putting leftover supplies into our cars, an older woman, one of the locals, walked by and paused for just a moment. With a waving motion of her hand towards the street and in a thick accent, she gruffly said, almost in exasperation, "Thank you," and kept walking down the cracked sidewalk. It caught me off guard, and Neal, too – we were both left standing there speechless. She didn't stop and make eye contact; she just said it as she was walking by, so I didn't even know if it was directed at us. Unexpected gratitude is the most valued, but often times unrecognized for what it truly is.

We looked at each other, smiled, and then laughed. Was

she thanking us, or just thanking God that something was finally done? Without asking, Neal answered my question: "I don't know, man. I just don't know."

I don't think we fully realized the effect we had on the immediate community. We were so excited about the things we were doing – the actual planning and execution of a successful event – that the impact to the community was merely at the back of our minds. Knowing that we made a difference beyond ourselves made it even more worthwhile.

Driving by on my way to get my phone fixed, I looked at the wall: graffiti; in the streets: trash; and on median: both trash and graffiti. But in the center of the bleak median is the last remaining effect of our service day: an overgrown bush that's an island of green in the asphalt sea full of metal boats. As mine floated by, I absorbed the fleeting scenery.

FOURTEEN

As I approached the next signal at Normandie Avenue, I anticipated the sight that signified the community that surrounded St. Vincent's. Barely visible to the untrained eye sits a little market within the confines of a traditional mini-mall of the 80s, minus the yogurt shop. To a car speeding by trying to escape to the Santa Monica Freeway, this little corner store could be just a blur of a wall nimbly painted with items that are sold within it. But it's more than that to me.

It may very well have been a liquor store at one time; it had the design and set up of what I knew to be one in a corner shopping center. The low shelves that now held Mexican candies and religious candles at one time probably held cases of Corona and bottles of White Zinfandel. The name said it all: Norman's Market. ("Never call it Norm's!" Dan insisted, "That's a diner that should not be mentioned… ever.")

When I first met Norman's, it had lost its liquor license

and was acting as a corner mini-mart that made keys, sold very little food yet many piñatas, and had one video game, "Heavy Metal Slug," in the front window.

Norman's is not a store that I would have normally frequented. The signs in the front window were all in Spanish, and it was located next to a Discount Tire Mall. True, it was located just across the street from my high school, but I'd have probably gone to the Sav-On down the street in an even less desirable neighborhood before I found myself perusing the small aisles of the nearby corner store. So how did I find myself knowing more about this store than I ever thought I could? I blame stage crew.

When I arrived at St. Vincent's High School as a freshman, I knew I wanted to be involved. At my Orientation in late August, the Dean instructed the incoming class of 300 freshmen that, "here at St. Vincent's, we don't like to see gentlemen that are only here from 8:10 to 2:30 — we want to see an active student body that takes part in the various clubs and activities that we have to offer." St. Vincent's prided itself on being an all-male college prep high school that turned incoming freshman boys into well-rounded "men for others" by the time they graduated.

Young, impressionable, and ready to take on the world, I took the Dean's advice and dove right into the extra-curricular life at St. Vincent's. Besides joining the service club and the school newspaper – and running for Freshman Class Representative – I sought to start my career in "The Industry" (what I had heard people all over LA call the television and film industry). With all the studios and celebrities and "Hollywood" around, I knew I wanted to get involved with that aspect of Los Angeles. And I knew I'd have to get involved with my high school's theater to "get experience" in "The Industry."

Now, my brother had been going to St. Vincent's for three years when I arrived on the scene, so I was familiar with the school and its theater. I had gone to all six shows in which he had participated since his freshman year. After each show, my parents and I would wait for my brother to emerge from the dressing room to congratulate him and his fellow actors. I sometimes got to see backstage and all the props stored away – that's what really amazed me. I wanted to be a part of the magic of High School Theater.

"James, is this your little brother?" my brother's fellow actors would ask as they came up to us after a show. "It's 'little James!'" the intimidating high schooler announced. "Are you going to come to St. Vincent's for high school? Are you going to be as involved and as cool as your brother?"

As if I was not intimidated enough by a tall, high schooler talking to me, the barrage of questions regarding my aspirations were just too much. An embarrassed smile formed across my face, and I stared blankly at my inquisitor. Thank goodness James was there to answer for me, "Oh, sure. He's gonna come here, and I guess we'll have to see what he wants to do then." I was glad to have a brother who could rescue me from public embarrassment.

And so, when I did eventually attend St. Vincent's, and I saw what I wanted to do, I did it. And "it" was theater (among other the things).

I decided to audition for the Fall Drama, *A Midsummer Night's Dream,* my freshman year. What was I thinking? Even in ninth grade, I was not the type of person who shied away from a new experience or adventure, but something about standing up with all eyes focused on me clouded my mind. Although at the time, I didn't realize it. I mean, I *had* been in little performances during elementary school. I knew I could do it, or at least, I thought I could.

Auditions were after school during the second week of school. I had been to the theater many times before, so it wasn't a completely new experience; but without a set, it was a hollow shell – somewhat intimidating. As I sat in the seats, alone, waiting, my organs started to constrict; the phantom was taking his cue.

Then, the director came out. She was a high school theater veteran herself, having directed the last seven shows at

St. Vincent's. Ms. Stein didn't look too intimidating as she calmly entered, her vacant expression absent of all emotion – no smile, nothing. This was nice to see since I felt like I was going to throw up. Just remembering how she looked when she walked onto the stage makes my stomach turn with uneasiness.

She walked to the front of the group and feigned a huge grin; she was on stage in her element. This was the first time I had ever seen her smile. I had to tell myself to breathe.

"Hey, everybody," she said with too much energy, smiling at the actors she already knew would be cast. "My name is Ms. Stein, and are we gonna have some fun today! We've got a great show to cast, and I think you'll all enjoy it. It has a large male cast, as well as many opportunities for the lovely ladies who've so graciously come to us from what seems like everywhere!" She fake-laughed and then abruptly stopped, and I breathed a little easier... sort of. If she was going to talk most of the time, I could handle that. She thankfully started up again.

"Now, I've got a bunch of copies of the script here – well, sections of the script – for you to all read over and then present. You need to get yourselves in groups of four and..."

I am not even sure if she kept talking after that or not. Outwardly, I assume I looked like I was paying attention; but on the inside, I was in a state of sheer panic. I was more anxious than I had ever felt. It was similar to the feeling I got the time my car fishtailed while I drove to school during the infamous El Niño rainy season. It was a wave of emotion that I never thought could result from the four words: "get yourselves in groups."

Everyone started to move. Some people went down to the front row to grab handfuls of scripts; others started moving towards a group of friends. I saw the only familiar faces get into their groups, and then all I saw were their backs. I was alone. They say when you're alone, don't panic. Well, I remembered this, so I immediately panicked.

The groups all around me were busy working on their scenes, and I'm sure I looked like the lost kid in the market looking for his mother: desperate. Then, from behind me, came a familiar, condescending voice that I knew oh too well.

"Are you okay? Where's your group?" My brother asked as he scooted by in the row of seats behind me.

"Oh, I'm okay," I lied. He obviously knew I wasn't, as his tone slightly changed.

"Ben, where's your group? Do you even have one?" This time he seemed more concerned, yet still annoyed.

And out of nowhere and without really intending to, I replied with the truth – well, the half-truth: "You know what? I don't think I am going to tryout today. I just don't really feel like it." My anxiety didn't disappear, but I faked as best I could that I was perfectly fine and that I had objectively decided not to audition. I did want to tryout, though, I really did – but I was just too scared to perform on command.

"Are you sure? This is all you've been talking about doing this since you heard about it." He knew what he was doing. I think he was 70% concerned and 30% covering himself so he wouldn't get reprimanded when we both got home and my parents learned that I hadn't tried out. He knew that they would've blamed him, if he had not tried (unsuccessfully) to convince me to tryout.

"No. I'm sure." I knew I had to leave that theater soon. I knew I wouldn't last just hanging out in the theater for the next hour while everyone around me was excited about auditioning.

"Alright. Well, we'll be done in about an hour," he said, walking back toward his group.

The fear and anxiety started to disappear as soon as I had verbalized my decision. And as soon as those emotions were gone, at their heels entered embarrassment. I was in awkward position: I was sitting alone, not doing anything that had to do with auditioning; my brother had to "help" me and had since gone back to his group where, I was sure, he repeated what had happened and made it seem like I couldn't handle myself. And third, I was still feeling the effects of the day's anticipatory anxiety on top of the past ten-minute's agony. I felt like I was about to throw up.

I quickly picked up my things as I discretely left my seat,

which was not discrete at all as the chairs flipped up in front of me as I exited the row. My high school career was crumbling before my eyes, and I didn't know of anyone to whom I could turn for support.

I opened the first door off the lobby, rushed in, and plopped myself down on a pile of curtains, using all my energy to prevent a life-altering public vomiting. I was so disappointed because I didn't follow through with what I had intended. Looking back, it was ridiculous; but at the time, what seemed to be the most important thing I was going to do with my high school career was over. Boo-hoo: I didn't have what it took to be in high school theater. I was devastated without having the chance to be rejected.

It was high school theater – and I could never be star in it: again, boo-hoo. I breathed deeply and systematically, trying to regain control of the situation. As the pain of self-rejection subsided, I saw two full-size Roman columns soar to the ceiling. Between them rested the lance from James's first show, *The Man of La Mancha*. I was in the prop room I had once seen but from the young, admiring theatergoer's perspective. At that instant, I had a whole new, disappointed perspective.

I got up and started to look around the room, finding a pile of dusty typewriters stacked under a crudely constructed table with bushels of silk flowers mounded next to a dingy chandelier. Faux marble boxes, fake food, mismatched place settings, broken chairs and knickknacks cluttered the storage space. All these things mesmerized me, and the space had such character that I wanted to touch everything. I picked up a dust-covered, resin paperweight that looked like it was from the '60s – something Mike Brady would have in his study. When I put it back, I realized my hands were covered in theater dust. I explored the items in the dark room, and if the sound of the actors exiting the theater didn't startle me, I might have missed my ride.

On the drive home, I said nothing and thought about how my decision not to try out was probably a good one. I decided I was glad I was not going to be an actor. The more time that passed from that decision, the surer I was that I had defaulted to the right decisions.

And my parents weren't upset at all, contrary to my prediction. They were puzzled, though, because I wanted to be involved in the plays so badly.

"Are you sure you're okay?" they asked.

"Yeah, I'm fine. I'll just do something else."

As it turns out, the following Monday, an announcement was made that the theater was looking for guys to be part of the stage crew. I had always enjoyed creating, designing, and building things, so I thought, "why not?" I knew I couldn't be on stage, but I knew I could play a vital role in creating it.

The first day, we all met in the same seats that I had sat in the week prior. Once again, Ms. Stein immerged from backstage as stolid as ever. She gave a condescending speech about the importance of safety, cooperation, and cleaning up, and how important the crew was to the show's success. This speech made more sense to me than the first one I had heard her give, and the only nervousness I felt was that she might recognize me from when I had not auditioned.

She introduced our Technical Director, Bill, who had graduated St. Vincent's seven years prior. Stage crew would meet every Wednesday and Friday afternoon and then on Saturdays. Bill discussed all the different aspects to the theater in which we could get involved. To me, scenic painting and props seemed like the most creative and fun. But that was the last I heard of them for while.

After about 20 minutes of introductory business and passing back forms, we all started to work. The crew veterans took new members as assistants and showed them the way to properly use a belt sander, rotor saw, drill, staple gun, matte knife, and most importantly, broom and dustpan.

In the first couple crew sessions, I tried to keep a low profile, pursuing different aspects of set production to see what I liked best, but committing to none. I liked construction because we were able to create structures that would become the set, but in the back of my mind, the prop room with its the hodgepodge collection of junk incessantly called to me. I wanted to work with set design and props, but no one mentioned it after that first day; and I assumed that a senior or junior was in charge of it.

I continued to work diligently and helped with whatever task they asked of me. I ended up cleaning out the tool closet, re-organizing the wood in the wood shop, and helping make flats (very simple, repetitive wood frames). Everything I did was new and, therefore, exciting; and I saw "just doing it" as a way to make a good impression on those in charge. I never complained about the menial tasks, even though I knew I was capable of more than housekeeping.

After the third week, the whole experience seemed to be the complete opposite of what I had hoped for. However, Bill and I had developed a fairly decent working relationship, and I felt more comfortable talking to him than the crew chief, an arrogant senior who had been in Stage Crew for four years, about the situation:

"Hey, Bill – I was wondering: what's happening with the props and stuff like that. Who's the one that's in charge of the furniture and wall decorations?" I was a little bit nervous asking such a naïve question, but it was a lead-in into my next, more formulated request.

"Well, right now, no one to my knowledge. You'll have to ask Ms. Stein; I think she's working on it with the crew chief." He motioned towards the director's office. My desire sank to the bottom of my stomach like too much tapioca: I was not thrilled about working with the crew chief, and I was still intimidated by Ms. Stein. "Why, you interested?"

"Yeah, I was thinking about it. I think I could do a pretty decent job at making them and keeping them organized."

"Yeah, I think you'd do a good job. You should talk to Ms. Stein soon, though, so you can get started if you are gonna do it."

"Okay, thanks." I walked away, not really sure if I wanted to go and talk to Stein or Brent, a jerk who also happened to be the crew chief. "I better," I said to myself in a low voice as

I walked out of the wings towards the office.

"Uh, excuse me, Ms. Stein?" I thought to myself, could I be more timid? My heart was racing.

"Yes, come on in. Whatdaya need?" she asked forcefully but sincerely.

"I was wondering – "

"Yes?" she asked impatiently. "What are you wondering about?"

"Well, I was wondering what was happening with the props that you talked about on the first day? I was, sorta, well, interested in helping out with that."

"Really? Excellent." She became animated, but seemingly preoccupied. "We need someone to do the props for this show – it's a great prop show! I've a great idea how we can get all the glowing orbs we need fro the final scene – we're going to make them! Do you…" she went on about how great it was someone wanted to do props and that I could be in charge of the props and take responsibility for them. In spite her overly excited but still pointless drivel, I still got excited. I was glad I had finally asked.

And so it was, that I became a member of the stage crew. For the next four years, I was involved in the theater, whether the others wanted me there or not, whether I played by the rules or not. I was a member of the crew when I could be, and no matter how little I was present during the set construction in the months prior to the show's opening, I knew I was a part of the show.

That first play, though, brought my first interaction with Fr. Hank, a quiet priest of whom everyone always spoke highly. When I met him, I knew why: he never said much, just a couple of words of direction and always a "thank you" or an "I appreciate your hard work." He was an inspiration, at the time, because in his subtle way, he made me feel like part of the theater family; he made me want to stay involved when it seemed that no one outwardly cared if I stayed or not. As scenic artist, he was responsible for the appearance of the set. I admired his work, and I admired him.

I met many others, friends, during my first experiences on crew: Tony, Dan, Nick, Bryan, and Adam. The list goes on, but these guys were like the ones before them and the ones that I later met: they wanted to have fun while they created a set that was remarkable for high school theater. Some wanted to continue with set design or technical theater in college, but for most, it was just a way to hang out with guys that like to build stuff and more obviously, destroy stuff when it was no longer needed.

During that first play and even the subsequent three, I didn't exactly fit in with the rest of the "crew guys." I was dubbed "Prop Boy," which did not bother me, but I was often excluded from crew activities. So, I worked in my small space, creating the little pieces of the set that defined it as a newspaper office. And because I had to work closely with the actors during the actual run of the show, I stood at a mid-point where I had to try to hold the respect of both groups. I guess I did okay since it was my first show and I had practically no direction. Like on picture night, when the cast is in costume and the crew, in coat and tie, no one told me about it. I showed up in shorts and pocket T-shirt and was unable to be in the cast/crew photo. I was the odd man out, again.

One activity that I made sure I was not left out of, though, was the Norman's "run." Every crew session, someone would collect money and make a list of drinks and snacks to get from Norman's. I would usually go with Tony or Adam because we'd talk as we walked past the neighborhood church and across the street, discretely commenting on the other passersby. The people were very eclectic and truly represented the area in which they lived. The contrast to the St. Vincent's students who came from the Palisades or San Marino was interesting, though most often unmentioned.

We would walk into the store and search for the treasures on our list. I usually ended up being the one to hunt for the drinks while the other guys would play Heavy Metal Slug. Sometimes, though, some of the neighborhood kids were already there, preventing us from playing. Two kids would set the compelling video game on two-player mode and, armed with tanks, grenades, and bombs, tried to kill and destroy as much of the opponent as possible. It was like a violent version of Nintendo's Super Mario Bros. or Gyromite.

And so, I became aquatinted – almost to the point of friendship – with the little corner store. It sometimes reminded me of my childhood in my parents' store; but more than that, it represented my time in the theater.

So, as I approached Norman's, I was reminded of the years I spent in the theater, both the good and bad. And as I passed, I noticed they had started carrying some new items: the wall out front was repainted with their new merchandise. That wall out in front changed almost as regularly as the sets in the theater just steps away.

FIFTEEN

I continued down the street towards the Westside, passing offerings by the Santa Monica Freeway to enter the speeding ranks that were taking advantage of a permissive God. I just continued on with my mission to get to the Cell Store. My money saving feat of purchasing from a non-corporate store seemed to be losing its charm.

So down the street I barreled. Of course, I hit every red light; it was almost inevitable. And if I did get a green light, I was usually behind a car that was taking a left hand turn – and on Venice Boulevard, there were no left-hand-turn lanes. I still had plenty of time to get my new phone and then to Pasadena. I could do it.

Now, as I left my high school behind, I kept focused on where I needed to go, but it was hard not to think about what I had left behind. I drove these streets for four years, the years when I really developed who I was. And it was no easy task.

78

Though technically inaccurate, Martin Short's explanation in *The Three Amigos* of the word *infamous* as "more than famous" was the true meaning of the word for me. *Infamous* is how my friends described me at graduation and for the three years prior. And I think this misinterpretation of a definition accurately portrayed me, even just after my first couple of months at St. Vincent's.

The real awaking came one day during my senior year when I was helping to collect the food for the "Shaka-CAN" food drive. I was bringing a bag of canned foods to the storage unit, and the bottom of the bag gave out, releasing cans across the walkway. An underclassman who had just dropped off his food stopped to help me collect the runaway canned goods. I did not recognize him, so I figured he was a freshman.

"Hey, aren't you Ben Grenaro," he asked me.

"Um... yeah. Why? How do you know who I am?" I was perplexed. I had absolutely no idea who he was, yet he knew my full name.

"I dunno. I just do. Everybody knows you."

"Oh," I said dumbfounded.

He turned and walked back to his own class as I headed to turn in my armful of cans. I couldn't imagine that all 1200 guys at St. Vincent's knew who I was, but they might have. And it all goes back to my first couple of months at St. Vincent's when my persona was formed by my classmates.

Unfortunately for me, no one told me that when you get to high school, you're not supposed to act natural. As a freshman, you are supposed to put up a facade and try to be something you are not. Since I failed to receive this memo, I approached high school with the energy I had carried with me as I left nine years at my Catholic elementary school. And thus, my reputation formed.

I didn't realize what had happened until later, but in hindsight, I guess it did start from the very beginning. It may not have been the best of times as isolated incidents, but if I had a chance to do it again, I probably wouldn't change things.

My first period on the first day of school, Algebra, was

taught by one of the coolest teachers at St. Vincent's, Mr. Goods. He spent more time talking about the best places to eat in LA than about the x-axis or negative integers.

"Oh, you're from the Valley?" he asked me in class when we were went around and introduced ourselves. "You ever been up to Killer Shrimp on Ventura? That's some good shrimp."

"No, but I know where it is," I offered. Mr. Goods and I hit it off from the start, and he was always looking out for me when the class tried to gang up on me... except during the fateful second week of school when I opened my mouth during a discussion about cooking.

Mr. Goods announced: "At the end of last year, I brought cooked barbecue for my class during lunch. If you guys are good this year, I'll see what I can do." Everyone started talking about foods and a party.

I eagerly offered, "Hey, I'll bring mashed potatoes if we have barbecue." And instead of leaving it at that, I added, "I make some mean mashed potatoes."

Well, that comment set off the class. The football players at the back of the room laughed, which forced the others to awkwardly join in.

"How mean are they, will they bite?" one guy mocked. "I'm scared of Grenaro's mean cooking!"

"There's nothing I can do to help you out on that one," Mr. Goods said sincerely with a sympathetic smile, "you're on your own." I laughed too, because I knew how lame it was to say. But I did really make good mashed potatoes; it was about the only thing that I *could* make. For the rest of the year, I never escaped the stigma of "mean mashed potatoes."

The second week ended, and at the time, I failed to realize the reputation I was building by being myself. I still thought St. Vincent's was the greatest place, though I started to notice that I didn't have any close friends yet.

"But it's early, mom," I had to explain to her, "I know that I'll start to find people who I can associate with and call friends." (Or did she say that to me?)

The third week was normal; I went about my routine

without incident. But the fourth week of school was as exciting as the second. During History, we were talking about a current event, and I always liked to participate in a discussion on a topic of which I had some grasp. We raised our hands and were called on in turn. My hand went up, I was called on, others would speak, and then I would have another comment. Up and down, my arm was flashing. My additions to the conversation were sound, but I learned another lesson about high school - the hard way - during that discussion.

"Well, just recently on TV, Oprah said that-" the class erupted in laughter.

"You watch *Oprah*?" a voice called out.

I honestly replied, "Yeah. Well, sometimes, if there's nothing else on. What's wrong with that?" I was disappointed that I was being so harshly judged by what I watched on TV. I'm just glad they didn't know I liked to watch *Star Trek*.

And the impression-forming first month was not over yet. Elections were the following week, and I suppose my overly confident attitude during my campaigning set my reputation in stone. I became infamous. And, apparently, you can never become *un*-infamous.

But that first year helped me to grow stronger as an individual at a time of conformity; my classmates didn't seem to like those who expressed opinions and ideas contrary to the accepted norm. The friends I did eventually make over the years were the ones who took the time to get to know me. And I still have most of those friends today.

Sadly, though, along with that infamy came a lot of guys who wouldn't give me a chance at first, let alone a second chance. I know I wasn't the average St. Vincent's student, but I wasn't *that* strange. So, when someone would push me in the hallway or throw an apple at my head or shoot a staple gun at me from across the theater, I wondered how it made them feel, what they got from it. Most of it stopped as soon as the guys got to know me, but with some guys, the barrage was unrelenting.

During our Senior Week, the teachers threw us a barbeque on the field. By this time, I would say less than a dozen of my 280 classmates were still holding onto the idea that I was some sort of freak as had been wrongfully established that first year. The punks, the surfers, the geeks, the skaters, the loners, the Eastsiders, Westsiders, and local guys – just about everyone had grown up and realized that different is good, except some jocks who verged on being spoiled rich kids. It's ridiculous how some guys don't grow up at all in high school.

When I got to college, though, people didn't pass judgment publicly, as they did during high school. But I was still as individual.

In my third year of college, I decided, in true form, to run for president of the student body... for fun. That was an experience in itself, especially since I was running against my roommate. I ran independently, without spending the allowed $300, but only put about 85% of my effort into my one-man campaign. During the last week of the two-week campaign period, a guy rode by on his skateboard and then doubled back when he saw me campaigning on the main walkway. I had no idea who this guy was, but he knew me and approached me as if we were long-lost friends.

"Hey man. Dude, you running? Cool."

"Yeah. Make sure you vote. Hey, how do I know you? I mean, where do I know you from? Were you in one of my classes this year?"

"No, man, we weren't in a class. I just know you. Everybody knows you. Dude, you're Ben Grenaro. You're a player, bro."

I was caught off guard; what was this guy even talking about? Not only had he said that everybody knew me, but he called me a player. Maybe everybody did know me. I'm not sure what I was doing that drew such attention, but it didn't work well enough: I lost the election (but at least I was consider "a player").

To be infamous, in my mind, isn't that bad. But I just wish there was a better word to describe it. Maybe I should start to say I was "well-known to the point of obscure notoriety." *Infamous* is just easier, as long as people are up on their Martin

Short films.

SIXTEEN

Though it was a weekend, high school-aged kids who looked older than I did were hanging out around the local community center. These were kids who lived in the neighborhood and probably attended the local public schools or were bussed out of the area to other public schools, which in turn bussed kids back into this neighborhood. I watched their interactions as I waited for a light to turn green: guys playing basketball, girls just hanging out on benches, and an occasional couple holding hands or each other.

Even though I'm just a few years older than they are, I wish I could understand – remember – what it was about high school that made it such a great time (at least for me). Maybe it's hindsight bias, but when I watched those kids and the way that their weekends were free, I was envious of their youth and freedom. None of them had to trek half way across the city to run unexpected errands. Or maybe they did, but those errands – to them – weren't frivolous at all. Maybe if they did have something to do, it was important or else they wouldn't be bothered with it. I may have a hard time pinpointing what it was about my high school experience that defined it, but to understand the average high schooler is not as hard for me now, as it might have been while I was actually in high school.

College gave me a whole new perspective on high school. It only took two simple occurrences to make me view high school differently. First, within the initial month of classes, I had an epiphany one night as I stared at books I had purchased but knew I would never open; St. Vincent's expectations were far greater than my college's. I couldn't believe how prepared I was when I got to UCSD, nor how some of the other students who had come from the "leading" schools in Stockton or Modesto seemed to lack the essential preparation to have a smooth transition into college. The second event that revealed a new side to high school was the job I got towards the end of my first year; and I have to say, it was a year about as typical as a ride down Wilshire in a double-decker London Bus.

Now, as prepared as I was to handle college, I don't know if I was completely ready to go to school with girls again, after being in an all-boys classroom for four years. Most of the guys in my class from St. Vincent's faced a challenge as soon as breaking free from parents and home and moving into the co-ed world of college: they went girl crazy and ended up in relationship trouble. I think I handled it fairly well in comparison to some of my peers. Pregnancy is not a cool thing while trying to learn molecular physiology. Then, there were a few, like me, who didn't differentiate the way they treated girls from the way they treated their buddies in high school. Big mistake.

Going to school with girls (finally) was an eye-opening experience, to say the least. It's strange the way guys that I had known from high school now acted differently around girls simply because they went to classes with them. Sadly, it took me half a year to realize what it meant to be "more than friends" with girls. But I didn't let that affect the way I acted or my college experience; girls would always be there, I figured, so I better do the things that are limited to college. So, as I simultaneously tried to learn about and understand women, I got involved with "college life."

After the first month of school, my college-assigned mentor warned me not to get involved with too many things, as he saw that I was joining every campus organization that looked interesting to me. "You can always do more later; you don't want to burn out in your first year."

Burn out? I hadn't even gotten warmed up yet. By the end of my first year, I become so involved in such a broad range of activities from campus TV to social committees to community service that I was nominated for a "Freshman of the Year" award. I was selected as the university's delegate to a regional conference as the most active and involved freshman. Sadly, I lost out before being passed on to the national level. It was between me and another guy from Oregon State who had similar experiences; the only thing that separated us: a fraternity. He was in one; I wasn't. So, I left the conference without being the regional winner, but I had an experience that was quite incredible for someone who was warned of burning out.

When I returned a non-victor, some of my friends told me that I should join their frat so that I could be more competitive in pursuing other awards and also because it would bring me close together with a group of friends that I would have for life. I told them I didn't really want to do something just to be competitive or for a resume. And as for that group of friends, I already had them. I realized early on that the guys who had attended St. Vincent's with me shared a bond that could not be formed during meetings, initiations, or parties that encompassed "Fraternity Life" at my school. We did all that and the philanthropy (which we called "Community Service) just by going to school. My high school did prepare me for college, but I don't think a person realizes what they're learning until they've applied it in real life. And college is the closest thing to real life without it actually being "real life." For me, it was almost like a practice period.

I think that practice was practically over as my freshman year wound down. In my last quarter of my freshman year, I knew I needed to get a job to replenish my diminished savings. Being social in college is expensive, especially when going to school with girls.

I searched for jobs online, but the electronic resume did not seem to represent me well enough. So, I started talking to people who worked on campus, both students and non-students, to see if any jobs were available anywhere. As a last resort, I approached my college's dean and asked him about the University-sponsored high school being built just off campus which would open the following September.

"It's its own deal. You should go ask the principal - they just hired her. But I don't have any idea of what's going on down there now."

So, I approached the little school, which was working

out of a temporary office that was the size of a small dorm room. Hesitant, I asked if they were hiring. I had a feeling that their answer was not going to be the one I wanted. I was right.

"Well, I wouldn't mind volunteering," I offered, trying to appear as if I wasn't just after the money they claimed not to have.

"Are you sure?" the principal asked.

I guess I was; I didn't have a job and the idea of being involved with a brand new, evolving school sounded interesting. So, I set up a schedule to work – no, to volunteer – twice a week. (My parents would gladly support my public service habit with extra funds, as needed.)

I worked at whatever they asked me: I was a gopher, a personal assistant, secretary, and a policy maker all at once. And I was the only one of the small staff of three that was anywhere near the high school age. As they developed rules and programs, they asked me for my input, so I was able to apply the things I had experienced at St. Vincent's – the good and the bad - towards this new enterprise.

This development of a new high school forced me to look at my high school experience objectively, to identify its essence. In doing so, I realized that my high school prepared its students for college more than most other schools. As I saw this new school materialize from an innovative idea, I realized that a school is more than meets the eye; consequently, I understood my own experience better.

I continued working at the school for the next two years as student activities coordinator. Whenever I wasn't in my own classes, I worked with the students in extra curricular activities, enhancing their education. From leadership to clubs to community service, I tried to allow the students to develop and realize their talents productively.

I hoped to make as much of a difference in their lives as they did in mine, but I didn't know for sure because I graduated and moved back to LA before that first class of 9th graders graduated. I wasn't asked to write any college letters of recommendation; I wasn't involved that three-days-before-the-deadline dilemma of choosing one school over another. But when I went back to their graduation, I saw students who seemed to be able to do anything. Some of the kids I had worked with went on to UCSD, while others went to Stanford, Berkeley, and one even went to Columbia University for pre-med. They realized their potential to reach college, but had they realized why they were doing it?

Those students, my first "classes," taught me about my own education, and I don't think I'll know if I helped them until they realize it themselves. And that won't be until they apply it in real life, maybe even beyond the "practice life" of college.

SEVENTEEN

I sat at a crosswalk, letting some of the slowest moving pre-teens cross the street. When they finally reached the curb, one of the smiling youths turned around and with his hand, made a gun shape, his thumb straight up and only his index finger extended. Then, he shot at me. He very casually took aim at me, a stranger, cocked his finger back and shot his very powerful, imaginary bullet at my face.

When the light turned, I accelerated casually, not waiting to see what he meant by his warm, universal gesture. I knew the neighborhood I was in wasn't the best, but I believed the people who lived there were people trying their hardest to survive the harsh world that was 21st century LA. This hand gesture caught me off guard, but didn't shake my belief about the community's good people.

In LA, the reputation of communities is secured by a few visible residents and accepted by the rest. Whether a kid in Watts thinks his neighborhood destined for destitution or an elderly woman in Bel-Air settles for economic homogeny, communities don't change unless people are willing to actively work for change. It's the same across the city: people have the power but don't harness it – they just let it slip through their pointing fingers.

Just down the street from my high school was yet another Catholic high school, an all girls school. According to one of the older priests who spoke as if he knew everything about education, religion, and the local area, this former convent was run by a group of disorganized nuns. (This was coming from the priest whose teaching techniques required the use of expletives and verbal assaults on the material being studied.) It was a small school, which had been on the verge of closing for 20 years.

As I passed by, two of the nuns were outside in habits, working in their garden, a common sight. They were probably some of the last nuns in LA who still wore the habit. Maybe they think that by wearing the restrictive headdresses, they are more respected. I'll be the first to admit, when I see a group habit-ed nuns walking around Disneyland, I can't help but laugh. But by this point in time in LA, a nun gets respect by being a nun, not by what she wears.

Nuns aren't new to me, but I think the nuns at my elementary school were not the run of the mill, habit wearers. I think mine were the new wave of nuns. And it's not that they are young, fresh, and straight from the nunnery either. No, the nuns that I had were over 60 but acted like they were 25. One in particular stands out in my mind as anything but a typical nun. But you can't have an eccentric nun without a Catholic school.

My elementary school was the desired school for the Catholic celebrities that lived in our part of the Valley. The weekly liturgies were counted as instructional time, and we had fulltime nuns as part-time teachers – two features missing from the public school that was located across the alley from St. Michael's. The Pope's picture prominently displayed in the foyer of the office set a different tone for my school, too. John Paul II kindly looked at the school children, inviting them to learn, pray, pray to learn, learn to pray, and pray some more.

In the fifth grade, I was fortunate enough to experience the religious stylings of Sr. Mary Henry (her nun name). As our religion teacher, she presented all the teachings of the church – some of which she truly believed, and others, with which she could not be bothered. A typically Irish nun that you would only find in LA.

She was a nun that did not fit the habitual mold, though. When she wasn't teaching or praying in church, I later learned, her "hobby" was acting as an extra in movies and on TV. She only did it occasionally, but she later revealed that she felt that was where she could have done her greatest ministry. I think I caught a glimpse of her – oddly enough, dressed in a habit in the opening airport scene in *Die Hard 2*, though she'd never confirm it. And if she wasn't in a movie, she often times acted as a consultant to The Industry, offering them an accurate account of nun-life… among other things. But Sr. Mary Henry truly did dedicate her life to God and serving others, and she was a teacher because she truly loved children.

She was the Sally Field of the nunnery – not *The Flying Nun* part, but the strong, independent woman. She did what she did for herself: Gidget without the surfboard, Norma Rae without the Union, the woman from *Places in the Heart* without a family. Sr. Mary Henry would have been the real-life nun that took parts from the Nazi's cars in *The Sound of Music*.

If you saw Sr. Mary Henry, you'd think she was your average nun; but her students knew the truth. Two distinctively "Sr. Mary Henry activities" made her legendary on the campus of kindergarten to eighth graders. First, she was known for wearing her "Hallelujah Dress" on days that were special. It was not an extremely special dress; in fact, it was never the same dress. The way that the students knew it was a "Hallelujah Dress" was that she would announce it to her first class of the day.

"Good morning boys and girls. I got up this morning, and I just had to wear my Hallelujah Dress today. Now, let's get to work." And the class would whisper about the reason she was wearing the dress.

Every time the rumor that she was wearing her "Hallelujah Dress" circulated at recess, her classes knew they were in for a treat. Sometimes, she would take the class outside for the period; other times, they would go over to the adjoining church and see the sacristy. The best time, though, was when she would bring videos into the classroom – if she showed a video, she always brought snacks. When Sr. Mary Henry was wearing her "Hallelujah Dress," she was always in a good mood.

The other thing that supported her reputation as a "rebel" was not her revolutionary belief that she would someday be the first woman priest, nor was it her Industry involvement, of which most people were not aware. Sr. Mary Henry was known by the older students as a table dancer.

When giving a lesson on miracles or the sacraments (and without any warning), she would get up on top of the tables or desks or chairs or anything that was higher than the ground and start to dance. Her dances were simple: a two-step or a twirl – but they always were uniquely "Mary Henry."

"Where'd you learn to dance like that?" Casey asked.

"Oh, back in Ireland we always danced," she responded with her Irish accent in full force. "My sister and I would get up on the table when mother was not looking. We just danced and danced." She would always dance on the tabletops when we were never ready for it, but she would never do it if we asked.

"Will you dance on the table?" Jill asked, giggling with embarrassment and excitement.

"What are you talking about," she would respond sternly. "I don't dance on the tables. Who told you that?" She would smile and then resume her lesson on the early Christians.

Her lessons always included stories that demonstrated her point. Usually, they were about being back in Ireland, growing up in the country. Her stories always started with "When I was a small girl back in Ireland," and always kept me on the edge of my seat. I liked hearing stories about people and their lives – it inspired me.

One story, I still remember vividly. As she told it, I imagined a green countryside, like the pictures I had seen in my *Child's First Book of Saints* book when they illustrated the St. Patrick story. I pictured a field of shamrocks and grass and lots of greenery. She told us how she and her sister found an old cart in a field and decided to take it for a spin. Together they labored to roll it up to the top of the hill that stood behind their little country home (where, I envisioned, all they had in the kitchen was potatoes and stew).

"My sister and I both got into the cart at the top of the hill. My sister told me, as we started to propel towards the barn, 'Hold on, and don't let go for any reason.' I listened, as the younger sister always does, and gripped the front of the cart even tighter. We inched along slowly at first; but then we leaned forward, and the wobbly cart started to pick up speed. We went down the hill at what seemed like lightening speed. We were just having the time of our lives when we realized we were not slowing down fast enough as the ground leveled out. We were headed straight for our old barn. Then, the cart seemed to move even faster, even though we weren't going downhill anymore. I looked back to see my sister had jumped out of the cart and left me there, heading straight for the barn doors. Can you believe it? She jumped out without any warning. By the time I looked back forward, it was too late, and I was too scared to jump out. And then... CRASH!" she yelled at us.

"I slammed into the old barn, and it collapsed around me and the no-longer-rolling cart. The next thing I knew, I was inside my house with my mother and sister leaning over me as I lay on the floor. My sister told me that I had crashed and she carried me back to our house. My mother had wiped off the blood that was covering my face. My sister was scared that I had died. Praise God, my only injury, besides some bruises where the cart poked me, was one scrape on the forehead. And what is truly miraculous is that it was shaped like a cross." She pointed to her forehead.

"And do you know what that scar represents, boys and girls?"

Thirty-five blank stares.

"Faith," she said dramatically.

I could not see the cross, but I believed her.

EIGHTEEN

You know how easy it can be to get distracted by the people and buildings you pass while driving on surface streets? Well, I've found these two prominent distractions to only be the ones that are most apparent. The driving diversions unrelated to buildings and people are truly incredible, if you can recognize them as such.

As I cruised west down Venice Boulevard, I began to notice that just about every telephone pole for seven blocks had a campaign poster on it, not one pole was naked. The political posters, just a little larger than an open newspaper, were printed in only two bright colors. These posters don't usually draw my attention, for yard sales, wedding expos, and gun shows always have their signs posted on the telephone poles. What really grabbed my attention, though, was that the small posters were posted from the ground to at least 25 feet up the pole. Forget quality, the sheer quantity (and placement) is what caught my attention.

I guess it wasn't that effective though, because I don't remember whose posters they were or for what they were running. But I've got give them credit for creative placement.

You know, it seems like every season brings an election to Los Angeles. And even if it isn't election time, someone is either promoting a candidate for the next one or still has their signs up in their front yard from the last one. It's like Christmas lights: by the time you get around to take them down, it is almost time to put them up again. With all the effort it takes to plaster the city with "Smith for Whatever" posters, why would anyone rush to take them down? Chances are, Smith will run again anyway...or his brother... or some other estranged cousin who wants to ride on the original Smith's coattails. Christmas lights still work even if a bulb or two are broken and the color's not so vivid.

Some of my peers aspire for political greatness in the

City and beyond; and I say, go for it – what could they possibly lose by trying... besides money? I'll do all I can to support them and continue to let them know I am available for political appointment.

Oddly enough, people around me continue to "let me know" how they cannot wait until I run for office. Friends, coworkers, and even people who I've only met once or twice will mention politics and my future.

"You know, Ben," a co-worker recently said to me, "Shala and I were talking this weekend, and we decided that you'd make a great politician."

"Oh, thanks. That's great – so now I'm a 'smooth talker?'" I responded semi-jokingly. I'd like to think of myself more like the Jimmy Stewart character in *Mr. Smith Goes to Washington*, rather than the politicos that wheel and deal in a not-so-ethical way.

"No, no. That's not it. We just talked about how you could really do some good for the community."

"Thanks – I guess."

I never really thought seriously about going into politics until Neal told me one day at lunch on one of his visits home from St. Louis, "I can't wait until I get to work on your Presidential Campaign."

"What?" I asked bewildered.

"I wanna work on your campaign. It'll be great – and it'll happen, too."

"Well if it does, you'll be there. Fear not... *everyone*'ll be there if I ever undertake a project that big."

The thing is, though, I tried politics, and my experience of succeeding and failing has convinced me that I really don't want the real thing.

It started when I was in grammar school - I wanted to be on student council from the time that I was able to run for a class representative position. For three years, I ran and was defeated by the popular kid elected: 34 of my peers did not have faith in me, an 11-year-old with a vision. Then, in sixth grade, I turned things around. I ran for Commissioner of Ecology, a position voted on by the whole school, and I won. I was in charge of the school's garbage; I was ecstatic.

I ran for and won another position the following year, but it was in my last year of elementary school I had a real victory. Even after a tumultuous seventh grade year where I had missed a tremendous number of school days because I contracted a rare, mild case of yellow fever, I was still elected as the school's Student Body President. Elected the first boy President the Catholic school had seen in over ten years, I thought for sure I would just move up the ladder of government forever. Even my coaches alluded to it at the football team's banquet: "Ben is cut out to be more of a politician than a football player." (I wasn't really a sports star – it had something to do with my dislike of having to blindly memorize plays that did not have any input from the players. Well, that and my aversion to taking orders from irate coaches). And I had assumed I had found the key to winning elections: be different; be real.

When I got to high school, I was unaware that the rules had changed. Remember, I had missed that conformity memo, so I think my individuality might have cost me the election.

Freshman elections were at the start of October, and I was confident that I was one of the best candidates of the seven who were running. With three positions open, whichever candidate got the most votes would be class president, and the two runners-up would be class representatives. I thought, for sure, I'd be able to secure one of the positions.

My campaign was simple: get my name out there, and people would vote for me. I spent an entire weekend making posters that were bright and colorful like the ones that I had used in the past to win a campaign. At a loss for creative, catchy slogans, I asked my mom to help me. Some might argue this was my fist mistake.

"You're in high school, now. I can't be coming up with your slogans - you have to do it on your own. I'm here to support you, but you have you come up with them." She was always trying to let me solve my own problems when I needed her help; and when I didn't need help, she was always there to offer it.

I came up with a few catchy blurbs, but nothing spectacular. So, my mom and I worked together to design the posters, and I was proud of the results while at home.

Early Monday morning, I confidently and eagerly walked onto campus and hung my posters prominently near the freshman locker area where everyone was bound to see them. I was more confident about my success now than I had been when I had turned in my signed petition and letter of intent. Then, I started looking at what the others had done for their posters – all of them looked the same, and none looked like mine. Mine were different...

The next day, we had an assembly where we gave our speeches. One guy humorously told about his past elected experience: "I was elected to be potty monitor in kindergarten – and I was really good at it, too." He got laughs and might have won, if he had not used "SEX" – just the one word – as his attention-grabbing slogan on all his posters. He was docked votes because of it. Catholic schools have somewhat strict rules about sex, you know.

Some of the guys were trying Student Government for the first time, and I thought they did a good job. Two of the guys were already popular though, because they went to summer school and were on the football team. They got huge cheers when they were called to the podium. Exaggerated popularity contests in the movies had materialized: a real life *Sixteen Candles*, but without Molly Ringwald. No girls, remember?

My speech was more mature than those of my elementary experience. I spoke clearly and confidently, assuring my new classmates that I was there to make a difference. I got a courteous response from them – courteous, at least, for 300 teenage boys. I tried to convince myself that the others got booed and heckled, too.

The following day, Wednesday, was the election. I tried to motivate – or begged, depending on how you define it – all the guys in my classes and in the halls to go vote for me. I was confident I could win.

Over the loud speaker at the end of the day, the Vice-Principal came on just before the bell was to ring: "Gentleman, I have the results of the freshman elections. Your new class president is Tom Dupkins." My heart sank as it raced. Two more spots, I thought – one must be for me. "And the two class representatives are Phillip Montrose and Fredrick Mites. Congratulations to all those who ran..."

He said something else, but I had lost interest. I put my head on my desk and then brought it up to focus on my teacher for the last minute of class. One of the guys who sat two seats behind me called forward, "What's wrong, Grenaro?" he said sarcastically, but without effect. I couldn't feel any more horrible. "You didn't think you were gonna win with posters like that, did you?" He rubbed his shaved head back and forth, laughing with half of the class.

"I don't know, I thought they were okay. Oh, well," I responded, appearing to shake off this comment as I had learned to do with so many of their jibes by that time. The bell finally rang, and I slowly left the classroom.

Who knew that when running for office in high school, especially an all-boys school like St. Vincent's, you should refrain from hanging creative posters if you want them to take you seriously? They were really effective posters – I still believe that... sort of. Actually, not at all.

Today, I'm quick to bestow the lesson I learned to any young person who is running for student government: "Blast off with Ben" written above a rocket does not go over very well with freshmen. And the poster with a palm tree on a small island was very creative, but it just didn't have the curb appeal that I thought it would. Creativity brought my political career to an end... for a while.

After that loss, I retired from student government until I reached college when I was asked mid-year to fill position for a junior who was appointed to an even higher position. That was my freshman year, and that half of a year was enough for me for a while.

The last time I even thought of running for an office was when I was in my third and final year of college. I was scheduled to graduate a year early, but I had made deal with my friend who had been involved with a lot of my Ben-ish schemes who still had to complete her fourth year.

"I'll stay my fourth year only if I win the presidency." So, at the last minute, I got a petition and signed up to run for president against my former roommate and three other candidates. No problem.

I told myself, and my parents, that I wasn't going to spend (actually, I think the word I used was *waste*) money on a campaign. If I was going to win, I was going to win on being Ben Grenaro. A lot of people knew me, and if I was meant to win, I could do it without "spending" a thousand dollars.

I campaigned on my own, everyday, for two weeks straight. I stood on the main walkway of campus, a path that every student walks to get to class. As it turned out, I knew more people than I thought, or at least, they knew me. I was never alone out there in terms of passersby, and strangers even became acquaintances.

After interviews with the campus paper that labeled me a "motivator," numerous debates, and days of self-promotion, I lost the election by a narrow margin for a campus of 15,000. But I am sure, just by informal polling, that those that voted for me would not have voted if I wasn't running: I had votes from transfer students in their forties, international students, and students who could care less. I even had the support of the non-voting university staff. I only lost by 200 votes, but that didn't bother me too much. I lost and my roommate won; so what, I was graduating just seven weeks later. The president, on the other hand, had to stay for his fourth year... and his fifth. See, because of his position, he wasn't able to finish all his coursework in just his fourth year. He ended-up staying for a fifth year and then some, I think. I was glad to be finished with school and able to start my real life.

I'm not sure if I could really ever run for office again, though. I've tried and lost; and I've tried and won – both ways work out. But, to make sure I am ready if D.C. ever calls, I've developed a slogan for my non-existent campaign. "Vote for a Change. Vote Grenaro." And of course, my mom would design the posters with a strategically placed rocket and palm tree.

NINETEEN

I merged onto San Vicente, still heading west, knowing very well where I was going: I was leaving the areas that were "east" of the Westside. I was entering the homestretch into Beverly Hills, soon to re-intersect with the Wilshire Boulevard that I had known about an hour earlier.

I knew that the communities through which I was driving - and those through which I was not - helped shape who I was. Spending most of my day in an office, I felt separated from the people, so when I was able to go out and drive and see things, I was sincerely interested. Some might label the areas I had driven through "tough neighborhoods" or "unsafe" or even "ghettos" (even I am guilty of this at times), but I really think that's just what people project towards the unknown. The more I was in an unfamiliar community, the more I wanted to know about it, and as I learned, the less hostile it became. LA functions as an entire entity, and to ignore one portion is to maim the city!

The road became more well-kept and the sidewalks, more landscaped as I approached the West LA/Beverly Hills area. I couldn't help but think what a little landscaping, some simple "greening," would do in the lower income communities that continue to edge closer to West LA. Trees can truly make the difference in the development of a neighborhood; a community can be more than its reputation allows.

Actually, I do most of my thinking while driving. The time alone allows me to really extrapolate an idea and let its tangents take hold, growing into an untraceable flowchart. The magic of driving allows for forgettable ideas that vanish almost as fast as they appear. Trying to write good ones down is difficult and unsafe; the car tends to swerve when I try to write, even if the pad is strategically placed on the steering wheel held by my wrist as I try to write and keep my eyes on the road. If the idea is really *that* good, I'll risk my life to scribble a quick note of the idea. Some ideas are worth the risk. But, then again, if the idea is just so different or memorable that I remember it later on, it tends to be the start of a new train of thought or, rather, "lane of thought."

I remember distinct thoughts or "think cycles" because they are habitual. I may not actually be remembering a specific occurrence, just a particular pattern in my thinking that I have recognized as reoccurring.

Generally, I know that when I drive south to San Diego, I always spend the first portion of my trip trying to figure out the fastest way to go. Would the 101 be open, or should I go around to the 5 via the 134; or should I take the 134 to the 210 to the 605 to the 5? The 605 to the 405 to the 5? So many choices to make, and only the surrounding cars and traffic can be used as gauges, unless you approach a juncture just as the clock turns 1:12 p.m. If you're lucky enough, you can use the "traffic on the 'ones'" from KFWB to steer you away from a particularly irate Freeway God. That split-second decision to stay on the 134 to the 210 changes the rest of the trip. And sometimes, when I see break lights as I pass the Eagle Rock, I think, maybe I should've just taken the direct route of the 5 instead of trying to wind my way around the radio-announced Sig Alert just before Knott's Berry Farm.

Aside from the ever-present traffic over the Sepulveda Pass, you really never know what traffic is going to be like while driving in or around LA until you are part of it. Once my route becomes fairly stable, usually around The Citadel (the former Goodyear Tire plant) on the 5, my mind drifts to other matters.

Most of my thinking is done on the streets and freeways of LA and those leading to and from San Diego. And driving south to my parent's house from LA is where I had one of those driving epiphanies.

I had finally decided to take the 134 to the 5 South on that Sunday afternoon. After the 5 winds away from the 10, every 75 feet, billboards loudly advertise things like The "World Famous" San Diego Zoo, The California Lottery, and this year's "Best Leading Local News Team for Southern California." This trail of signs continues past the Commerce Casino and down into Orange County until Knott's. Like the first leg of the trip does, these images always make me think of the same things: my parents' store and the advertising that we should've been doing to make sales increase.

That particular drive happened to be during the hectic summer before my senior year in high school. Heading south on the 5 after over a month of being away, I was ready for a vacation from my summer vacations to the East Coast and Europe. I had been going non-stop since school got out, and now, I could finally just rest for a weekend before going back to my parents' store in LA.

My BMW had supported me well for the ten months prior, and I welcomed the 100-mile trek southward after not being able to drive for over a month. I stayed towards the left, whizzing past the "slower traffic keep right" cars. The Freeway Gods had apparently taken the day off and let me have full control. With no set arrival time, I was free to travel at my own speed, not having to adhere to someone else's speed preference. I was the one in control of my short trip, and I focused on being unfocused.

As I continued on to San Diego, my mind drifted past the signs and the store and then focused my, then, recent adventure in Italy. I thought of the ice cream, the gelato, which I had had at least once a day. I thought of how smart I was to spend my "tourist money" on consumable treats rather than clunky souvenirs that I would have to lug back to LA for my parents to put away in a closet only later to be sold at a garage sale or given to the Salvation Army. I carried my souvenirs back to the US, though: I think I gained at least five pounds in three weeks, and that doesn't even include the pounds I shed by walking all over the European continent.

My thoughts then turned to the last night I was in Italy – Florence, to be exact. With an excess of Italian money that I wasn't going to be able to use the next day in France, I went with my friends to a gelato shop just walking distance from our hotel (which was ironically called *Eur Hotel*).

"Go ahead," I told Neal and Favio, "My treat; have whatever you want. I got it."

"Thanks, man," Neal said, as I paid for both scoops.

"Hell. Everybody - let's go. My treat: order what you want to celebrate our last night in Italy and our last night with gelato."

Shifting back to the reality of the 5 South, I looked to the side of the road and said out loud in a panic, "Hey what happened to Disneyland?" I looked to my right, then scanned ahead, and then looked back. I held an annual pass to Disneyland, and whenever I passed the snow-capped Matterhorn sticking out from the otherwise normal Orange County landscape, I knew I was about half way to my parents'. I had passed it while in deep thought, as proved when I saw a sign for the Santa Ana Zoo. Thinking sometimes takes me from reality without my even knowing it.

I started to then think about all the friends with whom I hadn't spent any time that summer because of all my traveling. I thought about how I really wouldn't have a chance to see too many of them in the short time that I'd be home before school started. The next week, I would start work: how could I possibly see them all, I thought.

"I should have a party. That's it: a party." I encouraged myself out loud. I looked around at the other cars self-consciously.

It was not a bad idea, though, to have a party and invite everyone I hadn't seen. I could invite enough people for a decent sized gathering, but it would get expensive if I was going to have feed everyone. And besides that, I wonder what people would expect at an almost-Senior's party. I had to make it different enough for people to come to without feeling like it was just a bunch of people sitting around having fun, even though that's what I would've liked to have happen. I thought of my different groups of friends: stage crew friends, school friends, elementary school friends, church friends – it would definitely be a unique mix of people. What kind of party could bring all those people together, though? I continued to pursue these thoughts, allowing them appear as I sped down the open freeway.

The next thing I knew, I was already flying past "The Nuclear Boobs" on a recently repaved and widened stretch of freeway. I had been concentrating so hard on my party planning that I had failed to notice that I was driving and maneuvering the traffic without really thinking. They say some people can't drive and do something else at the same time; well, I can drive and think – no problem. It almost heightens my reflexes, though being entranced in such a state prevents me from accurately self-reporting on the phenomenon.

I was almost at my parents' house, but I hadn't figured out the main theme of this inevitable party yet. After rejecting the idea of a poetry party (too intellectual), from nowhere, Italy appeared in my head again: gelato. I thought of having an Italian ice cream party, but never saw gelato in the US. Then, like light at the end of a long, dark tunnel, I saw the answer: ice cream. My train of thought chugged through that tunnel at full speed; I stayed in the fast lane.

"Perfect! What could be better?" I said as if I was upset that I did not think of it sooner. And it was perfect: most people love ice cream. In the heat of August, it was just unique enough to make people want to come to a party that would dare to exclusively serve the dairy dessert and its derivatives (smoothies and shakes). But I thought it was still missing something to really make it unique. It needed something else... something uniquely Ben. I thought I could charge people, like parties that have other "specialty" refreshments; but I couldn't see charging my friends as they came to my door.

Thinking of all the stuff that goes on an ice cream sundae, trying to figure out how much everything would cost, I thought of the amount of whipped cream and chocolate sauce and cherries and sprinkles that it would take. Then, as I was watching out for possible dust clouds as I maneuvered the 5 through Camp Pendleton Marine Base, the party idea evolved once more. I would provide the ice cream, and everyone could bring a topping to share: a potluck. The idea of the party consumed me for the rest of the ride.

As soon as I got to the house, I pitched the Potluck Ice Cream Party idea to my mom for immediate consideration and, hopefully, approval. I told her that I would take care of the whole thing, and that it wouldn't get out of hand. She posed questions of feasibility, and I was able to deflect her denial of my party. I told her I would take care of everything if she would let me have it at the house in the Valley. She agreed, after a brief parental consultation with my dad.

My mind focused on the party once again as I drove back up to LA two days later. I mentally reviewed the guest list five different times by the time that I saw signs for Disneyland. I thought of all the flavors I would need to get, and the decorations, and the toppings to suggest, and the invitations, and the mixers to get people to mingle. I just knew it would work.

A month later, when I was cleaning up after the party, I knew I had come upon a social gemstone. The party turned out great. The invitation was witty and even caught the attention of a number of my friends' parents. Shirley's mom even called and asked me if it would be okay if she came and helped in the kitchen. I was caught off guard, to say the least. People must love ice cream, I thought as I drove back from Thrifty's with an assortment of 17 different flavors.

For the most part, everyone invited attended. A couple of people were out of town, and others had other engagements but came late anyway. Some people who were not invited even called to see if they could come. In the end, over 50 people came from all over the city, from each of my different groups of my friends.

And as the guests arrived, so did the toppings... and oh, how they came. Whipped cream came from the West Valley;

Hershey's syrup, from Hollywood; fresh strawberries, from Manhattan Beach; Bozo brand rainbow sprinkles, from Glendale; brownies, from Pasadena; and cherries, from the South Bay. I'd tell people to bring one can of whip cream, and they'd bring three. Or, I'd tell one friend to bring some M&M's, and he'd bring two three-pound bags. At the end of the evening, I felt like I'd fed five thousand and still had 12 basketfuls of leftovers.

And what started out as a way to see all my friends before I started my senior year of high school has turned into an annual event that continues to grow each year.

Each year since, summer in Los Angeles has brought with it the Annual Ice Cream Party. Friends that I only talk to and see once a year look forward to it, revealing that they only see high school friends while at the Ice Cream Party.

And it has grown since it's humble beginnings. I continue to design an innovative invitation each year that is sent out to over 350 families directly, but after the third year, I no longer had it at my parents' house: the gathering became too large. In the past four years, I've had it at a hall, a conference center, and just this last year, we started holding it in a hotel in Eagle Rock. It has become quite the social event of the summer.

The possibilities are endless when there is time to think. Now, if I had a chauffer, I might be able to have the buzz of driving and still be able to safely write down the tidal waves of thought that I try to ride to shore. Right now, though, I continue to chase the surfboard that usually gets away from me before I even have a chance to stand up.

TWENTY

By this point in my ride, I had not really forgotten what had happened earlier with my phone, but I'd encountered a few distractions along the way that diverted my attention. As I continued to drive west on San Vicente, I left the urban city of

Los Angeles and entered the urban suburb of West LA and the suburban city of Beverly Hills.

As it was a Sunday, and as is the case in many places throughout the metropolis on Sundays, the street was lined with Star Wagons for a filming in a neighborhood just off the main boulevard. The crew was swarming around the sidewalks and trailers and tents erected to serve the union workers. As I came to the heart of the production, one of the side streets was blocked off, and I noticed a Beverly Hills cop (sadly, not Eddie Murphy) was leaning against his motorcycle "supervising." Yet another set in LA.

Sometimes it seems as though Los Angeles is just a big movie set and all of the residents are just bystanders, extras. And oddly enough, I think a lot of people end up as extras. Most of the time, we're not paid, but we get captured on film either through school or work, or just because the news makes us a part of the magic.

It started for me when I was in sixth grade; I was on *Beverly Hills 90210* as an extra. The filming was at a church in Hollywood, but it wasn't a big deal, though; I don't think I even saw the episode until it went into syndication years later.

I don't consider myself star struck like those who obsess and faint when ever they come within 200 yards of a celebrity. People from outside LA always ask if we see lots of "movie stars" when we're in Hollywood. They think that if you go to Hollywood and Vine, movie stars will be walking around and shopping in the stores. Sadly, they probably think that Hollywood still looks and operates as it did when Lucy and Desi decided to take the rest of nation to the entertainment capital of the world. Hollywood is more of a myth, now – the last bits of the Studio Era glory days are perpetuated by Johnny Grant, the community's honorary mayor who presides over the star-placement ceremonies on the Walk of Fame. Sure, there's been a recent movement to bring back the magic, but the stars are now found in and over the surrounding hills.

As a child, I never realized how close the movies were to me. My parent's store brought many celebrities into our lives, so I eventually stopped becoming really excited when I saw Jennifer Aniston driving up the street or Christopher Hewitt (you may remember him as the lovable butler, *Mr. Belvedere*) at a church function. I still was open to encounter someone famous, I just didn't feel like it was the best thing that had ever happened to me.

I used to think that because I grew up in the city, I was desensitized to some of that allure so compelling to others. Just because you're immersed in The Industry, doesn't mean you're not easily affected by it.

Take Adam's mom, for example; her husband works in The Industry, and yet, celebrities still mesmerize her. Specifically, she loves Tony Danza. She would not go out on Thursday nights when *Who's the Boss?* was on. A very Catholic woman, she would light candles every night for Tony when he had his skiing accident. She also religiously wrote letters to the network every time one of his shows got cancelled.

When we spoke of The Boss, usually in jest, she would always seem to find a way into the room.

"You mean, Tony, right?" she'd ask seriously. "Yeah, Angela always thought she was in charge, but we know it was Tony. Even Mona knew it."

She never caught on that we were talking about Bruce Springsteen and not Tony Danza, but we never wanted to hurt her feelings.

She was even the self-proclaimed president of her own personal chapter of The Tony Danza Fan Club. She never held meetings, but would always tell people her role when they commented on her impressive Tony Danza film collection. I think she had every episode of every one of his shows on tape. And she'd even send "president's newsletters" to all her friends a few times each year regarding the career and life of Tony Danza. Some women collect Lladros or Hummel figurines; Mrs. Ginn collected Tony Danza.

Mrs. Ginn was a regular mom, too, who worked as a secretary at a local school. She was as normal as they come; she was just unbelievably star struck, especially when it came to

Tony Danza.

Living in LA does make a person watch movies and TV shows differently, though. I watch the images on the screen, not as an escape from reality, but as an extension of my real world. The background shots used to establish fictitious settings are familiar places around the Valley and Greater Los Angeles. I was watching a rerun of *Charlie's Angels* on cable, and the convent at which they were doing some investigation was actually a local high school. And in one of the episodes of the *Brady Bunch*, Cindy's school is actually the public school my brother attended before he moved to our Catholic school in the third grade. But it's more than just schools; storefronts, malls, street corners, and our favorite restaurants are all in the movies and TV. My dad's liquor store was even in an episode of *Hill Street Blues* where they had to replace his windows with sugar-glass because the scene required a liquor store window to be shot out.

Whenever I see a movie or TV show, I try to figure out if I know the real location where they filmed it. I can't stay focused just on the film as a form of entertainment, but I want to know how and where it was filmed. *Seinfeld* takes place in New York, but they filmed it in LA; and whenever they do an outdoor shot, I think, "I wonder if that's Universal?" I'm familiar with the back-lots of the studios, so even they sometimes look familiar. I guess it would be like being from Chicago and watching *Ferris Bueller's Day Off*; if you are familiar with the city, you can't help but feel a direct connection to the film beyond the fictional story.

I get a sense of accomplishment when I can identify a familiar place on the big screen. The images connect with me, and I feel like The Industry is within my grasp. Having the studios in my backyard makes me feel like I am part of the "Hollywood Magic" or 'Valley Magic" or "Burbank Magic," depending on your perspective and the production.

I felt this connection whenever I had to make a video project for class, which seemed to come about at least once a year starting in the fifth grade. Teachers always wanted us to film a short movie for class to demonstrate our understanding of a novel we had just finished reading. The assignments changed slightly in high school, but it was still a movie. Instead of making a video for English class, we had to do it for History class.

During my freshman year, I had to shoot a video presentation about Tanzania with two other guys. Our mission was unspoken, yet understood: make the best video in the class. Doug filmed; I wrote the script; Adam provided the costumes and sets. Well… his dad did.

Mr. Ginn was one of LA's leading location managers and was able to get us props and costumes that far surpassed anything we could have dreamed of making or buying. Full headdresses and authentic attire transformed us into realistic Tanzanians. But more than the costumes, we were able to film in a jungle setting.

Now, no matter where you go in LA, it is hard to escape the urban city. (Sure, you could travel to Griffith Park to surround yourself with nature, but the Frisbees and birthday parties purvey the city.) The studio back-lots of Warner Brothers or Universal have lush areas that recreate any location in the world, but other, less elaborate sets also exist on smaller lots. And that's where we went.

When the time came to film our video, I was ready. It was going to be great; I envisioned an episode of *Travels with Chuck Henry*, which transported a local newscaster to exotic places to give an entertaining overview of it. I'm not sure if the newscasters in other cities had their own production companies that allowed them to do their own projects, but in LA, everyone seems to have a project (and an angle) that they are working. My project was for school, but I almost thought of it as a sample of work that the producers on my block might see. I wanted it to be as professional as three freshmen with a camcorder could make it.

We met at Adam's Burbank home in the morning, and started talking about our ideas. We were going to open with narration and still shots from a travel brochure that Doug brought. Then, we shot an interview with a snake expert. We decided that the snake should turn and attack the camera at the end of the interview – we thought that would be hysterical. (Why?) That all filled about three minutes of video, and then, we were at a loss. We had at least ten more minutes to fill.

"We need something more. Something bigger," Doug said with a distant look in his eyes. "We need something that is going to make it really interesting."

"But don't forget," I reminded him, "that we still have to include nine more facts to meet the 20 fact requirement."

"True. But don't forget that I have that video of *Jeopardy* that gives us five facts instantly." Doug, with his fine-tuned foresight, had taped *Jeopardy* when he saw that Tanzania was one of the categories the week before. It turns out that all of the "Tanzania" questions were selected in a row, so the clip could be used without other facts thrown in about "Famous Titles."

"How can we fit that in without making it seemed forced?" Adam finally spoke up.

"Well," I said, "now this is only a brainstorming idea, but we need to somehow make it so that someone in the video is watching television and turns to it to and sees the *Jeopardy* episode and then watches it as we film."

"Okay, but what's the setting?" Doug asked.

"Well, we talked about safari when we first were planning, let's actually go on safari. Ya know; send a group on safari into Tanzania. I know we said we wanted to do a promotional video, so why not show clips of a safari?"

"Okay, Ben, but where are we gonna to film it? We need a natural setting. Adam, do you have any strictly natural, vegetational areas around here? A park or something?"

"Yeah, sure. Johnny Carson Park is just a minute or two away. That could work." Now, being freshmen, none of us drove yet; so we would have to ask Adam's parents to drive to the park and wait for us to be creative – which could take a while.

"I don't know," I said. "Maybe there is a place out back we could do it. You have those plants alongside your pool, maybe that will work. I don't really want to ask your parents to drive us somewhere."

"Okay," said Doug, "let's go take a look outside and see what we can find. If it works, fine." Adam agreed with a nod of his head, and we moved our discussion outside.

"Okay, let's see," I said to no one. I thought about how I was lying to myself if I thought this is what I envisioned in our video. Our discussion turned into an argument over how we would film in this setting. Fortunately, Adam's dad interrupted us before we got angry with our "creative differences."

"I heard you talking about filming in a jungle setting. Do you want me to drive you somewhere? I can, if you want." He was making himself available to us; how could we refuse?

"Yeah, that'd be great. But where should we go?" I responded.

"Dad, we want to film a safari. Do you know anywhere around her where we could go? I thought maybe Johnny Carson Park, over near NBC," Adam seemed to be more productive and involved when his parents were watching.

"Well," Mr. Ginn paused as he thought, "I could take you guys over to Radford. They've got an outdoor set there." I thought how cool it would be to film on a set at a real studio. "Yeah, it's where the old *Gilligan's Island* lagoon set is. It's just sitting there."

"Wait. What? *Gilligan's Island*! Really? You can do that? And we won't get in trouble? Don't we need permission to do that?" I was intrigued with the idea. True, celebrities don't really affect me, but sets are another story; they are tangible symbols of creative genius.

"Cool," said Doug with a smile. "Let's do it."

"Okay, I'll meet you in the car in two minutes."

"Yeah," I agreed. "This is going to be awesome. *Gilligan's Island*. Wow."

"I told you my dad can do things," Adam offered.

"Yeah, but you never said *Gilligan's Island*. I mean, do you realize what we are doing? We're going to film a movie on the set of *Gilligan's Island*. How many groups are going to do that? This is so cool." I think being only 15 also contributed to the reason why I was so excited about filming on the lot.

Over 30 years after the final episode of *Gilligan* was filmed, I came onto the scene as the Gilligan of Tanzania. Okay, so I didn't mess things up like the lanky sitcom star, but I ran to the lagoon's edge and yelled, in Bob Denver fashion, "Skip-per."

We got down to business as soon as we set foot on the "island." We filmed scenes of explorers walking through the jungle and sitting at a camp around an imaginary fire talking about the natural environment of Tanzania that surrounded us. If you watch the final video, you can see some studio buildings on the edge of the screen. But, we still got an A for our dramatic representation of a Tanzanian safari. And even if I had failed the project, the creative process made the whole endeavor worthwhile.

You see, after that day of filming, I no longer watched the re-runs of *Gilligan's Island* as a viewer. I watch them with the perspective of an Island dweller. "I've been there before," I say to my sister whenever a shot of the lagoon comes on. When their ship sets ground on the shore, I know that it really wasn't all that uncharted, and the concrete LA River flows just 20 yards behind that shore.

TWENTY-ONE

I turned onto Wilshire again, and entered the heart of Beverly Hills, passing Restaurant Row on my right. You know, it's really surprising that this block or two of street is so acclaimed, when the restaurants really aren't the best of LA. Sure, they have Lawry's for prime rib and Bennihana for Japanese food, but both cost more than most people can afford.

The one restaurant on the Row that I would have frequented before it closed was Ed Debevic's. It was a 50s style diner where the food was okay, but the service was horrible, and that's what made it great. The serving staff harassed patrons and was rude when you took too long to order. I don't know why it closed.

I first learned of Ed's while watching KTLA's Morning News Show's fifth anniversary special. They held it at the restaurant, and the atmosphere looked different than any restaurant I knew. At that time, when I was still in elementary school, I had no idea where Restaurant Row was, or even how far I was from Beverly Hills. Back then, my world was the Valley. Then, in high school, I started driving and found the place one afternoon. I used to go whenever I want to have a fun lunch or dinner with friends because it was fairly central to both the Valley and the Westside – why did it have to close?

Anyway, there was this one waitress that symbolized that restaurant. Her "waitress name" was Princess Isabel, and she was an aspiring actress, as most servers there were believed to be. Every server had their own shtick that defined them, and hers was "selfish princess waitress from the '50s." She never had a smile and was always sarcastic, but Princess would instigate entertainment from the other servers and customers. She'd call out across the restaurant, "Hey, Betty Lou! Could you come over and serve your table, they've been waiting forever?" She was rude but concerned, if that's possible.

The last I heard she had been doing some stand-up comedy at the Comedy Store and not working so much at the restaurants, since every time she'd start working at one, it would close. I think a lot of people that worked at Ed's hoped that it would lead to something better; Princess found something better for herself because she worked at a place that allowed her the freedom to be who she wanted, even if it was just an act.

If I wasn't trying to get to the phone place and then out to Pasadena, I might have cruised by to see what new restaurant had come in as the next hopeful, "in" place. I kept on my course, familiar with the roads because of the route Jason took when he drove the carpool home during sophomore year at St. Vincent's.

Back then, I would sit in the back seat, with the subwoofer close enough to touch and spend my ride thinking, planning, or doing homework. The 30-minute ride to and from

Studio City to school was never wasted, even if just staring out the window, understanding the city through which we sped. I learned the names of streets of Beverly Hills, admired the homes and estates that lined them, and realized how exaggerated Aaron Spelling's show really was (and wasn't, at times). The sign that heralds to cars as they enter the city from Coldwater Canyon is not the world famous "Beverly Hills" Sign, but a small white sign welcoming commuters to Paris's Sister City. The gilded dome of Beverly Hill's Civic Center epitomizes the affluence the city oozes.

And almost daily as we twice drove through the gilt town, we happened upon – on one street or another – a woman who we endearingly named "the running lady."

At some point, adventure and ambition stop, and extreme, over-the-edge behavior begins. The running lady of Beverly Hills has ignored and run that stop sign. Like Forest Gump, but seemingly crazier, this woman could be found just running through the residential foothills of Beverly Hills almost everyday. Rexford, Sunset, Crescent, Santa Monica, and the surrounding grid were her stomping grounds, and passersby accepted her as part of the scenery – at least we did.

Some days, almost by some strange cosmic coincidence, I would say, "I wonder if we're going to see the running lady?" Then, I would repeat myself so that the guys in front could hear my question after they turned the music down. And then, almost out of nowhere, she would appear, huffing down Crescent Drive: her thin, gangly body jogging along at an unbroken gait. Her mouth never formed a smile – her pursed lips controlled her pace. Her vacant eyes focused only on the sidewalk in front of her, and she ran. That's all.

She was tan and leathered from running everyday in the Southern California haze, making her look at least 50 years old. Her daily attire was simple: a tight-fitting "I (heart) NY" shirt and black Spandex shorts. She didn't look happy as if she was finally losing those holiday pounds; she just ran.

It got to the point that – in seeing her run – Paul (the guy whose parents could actually afford to live in Beverly Hills) became annoyed with her. He would see her from the passenger seat and question her sanity.

"Why does she do that *every*day? Isn't she bored by now?"

He would almost get upset at her for having no real purpose. She had no apparent destination – just run around the residential foothills of Beverly Hills. We saw her on different streets, but never in any particular pattern.

"I don't know," I'd respond from the back seat. "Maybe she just likes to exercise."

"No. Richard Simmons likes to exercise. Billy Blanks likes to exercise. She is not exercising; she is just being crazy." Jason would laugh at the unfounded contempt that Paul held for this woman.

Paul had absolutely no patience for her by the middle of the year. As we were dropping him at his house one day, the running lady was jogging by across the street. Paul gritted his teeth and spoke through them: "why does she DO that? Everyday!" His last word was drawn out in disgust. He lugged his bag out of the car; and as he slammed the car door, I heard him yell to the runner who was now about three houses down, "Stop running!" in an exasperated voice. She didn't turn or falter, and he just stared at her in frustration. He huffed, turned, and then ran into his gated estate. And she kept running. Maybe she didn't hear him, though nothing covered her ears and she was well within earshot.

The next day, no mention was made of his unrestrained comment; it was an unsuccessful call to stop. Maybe she was forced to run as part of a curse left over from the Reagan Era, or perhaps she was trying to undo a curse; or maybe she was just trying to stay fit... everyday... without stop – who knows? She was as visible in the small residential area as Angelyne's billboards were to the rest of LA. And she was that ridiculous, too: we didn't know why she was there or what she represented. But her presence was known.

She ran without apparent purpose. No destination. No end goal. No explanation.

TWENTY-TWO

Down Wilshire at Santa Monica Boulevard, well past the Miracle Mile, the museums, and Rodeo Drive, I came upon the Beverly Hilton Hotel. Though less publicly glamorous than the Beverly Hills Hotel, it hosts a slue of civic and cultural events. The Golden Globe Awards are held there on occasion, as well an annual brunch for Catholics in The Industry. But for me, the most interesting event that I attended was a convention.

When I was 12, E.T. scared me, and I hadn't seen any of the *Star Wars* movies. Because my parents forced me to play sports at school, I think, the television became my comfort zone. In hindsight, I'm glad they made me play on a team for four years because it gave me time to hang out with my friends and made flipping the channels even more enjoyable.

My afternoons were spent relaxing in front of a glowing TV; sometimes, I even did my homework as I watched. Watching *Animaniacs* and the Four O'clock News on NBC with Kelly and Paul (though I preferred Chuck and Colleen) was how I spent my free time before dinner, before high school, before I no longer had free time.

In the evenings, my parents usually took control of the television, watching game shows like *Wheel of Fortune* or *The Love Connection*. But on Wednesday nights, the TV was mine. They knew from nine to ten that I would be watching "my" show: *Star Trek: The Next Generation*.

I have no idea how it happened; one night, I just flipped to Channel 13, and there it was. I got hooked on the show during the last episode of the first season, and for the next six years, I was a true fan – a Trekkie, if you will (although about half way through my devout following, my title was changed to "Trekker"). I had found a show that was my absolute favorite.

I considered myself a fan of a few shows like *The A-Team*, *The Simpsons*, and *The Golden Girls* (you have to admit, the Sophia character was funny), but *Star Trek* was a completely different kind of experience. Some might say I got caught up in all the hype that surrounded being a fan – I'd have to agree.

More than anything, I enjoyed the show for its complex stories, props and sets, character development, and message about humanity and society; but slowly, other fan-related activities began to seep into my life. I became a collector.

After getting two of the *Star Trek* action figures for Christmas that year, I started purchasing the rest of the series when I would see them at a good price. I liked to collect things, but I would never pay outrageous prices for something that, as a toy, could be purchased for about five dollars. For over three years, I bought the new figures as they came out so that I could make sure I had things to put in storage when I got to college. *Star Trek: TNG* figures were just another thing that I liked to collect – but the "figures" part was soon dropped, and *Star Trek: TNG* was what I collected.

Okay, so a middle school-aged kid likes a TV show and collects the products that go along with it. This would be normal for a regular show, but *Star Trek* had a history spanning three decades when I came on board. I soon started buying the official magazine, videos, coffee table books that explained technology in the 24th century, and even *The Klingon Dictionary* to learn how to speak the language of the aggressive aliens (I now only remember how to say "You have no honor"). I was immersed in the culture that was *Star Trek*.

"You know, Ben, be careful what you put in there," my mom said as I was starting to brainstorm ideas to put in my application essay for St. Vincent's. "I read an article that said admissions people don't look highly on people who put down that they are big *Star Trek* fans." She was overly concerned about my application even though I knew my records showed that I would be a fairly decent candidate for the school.

"Okay. I wasn't going to," I replied, slightly confused. Then, I said just to make her realize how lame she was being, "But I'll mention it in my interview if they ask me what is most important to me."

"Just don't say that your dream vacation would be to

116

spend it with those guys with the big foreheads. What are they called: Klintens?"

Her joke and mispronunciation made me laugh. "Klingons, mom. Kli*ng*ons. Don't worry, I am not *that* obsessed with it."

I'm not sure what gave her the impression that it was my entire existence, but just because I might like something a lot, but that does not mean I want it to be the only thing that I am about. Sometimes, people connect you with one thing and then are unable to let you exist in any other form.

Okay, maybe she got the idea about an obsession from what had happened that fall. As my birthday approached that year, so did a *Star Trek* convention in LA. I mentioned that I might be fun to go to instead of having a party.

Because both of them worked, my parents tried to figure out how I could go. They asked relatives, teachers, any one that even mentioned something that had to do with *Star Trek*. No one was able to take me, so I figured I wouldn't be going. In compensation, my mom spent a little extra and bought me the *Star Trek* uniform to wear on Halloween. So, I wouldn't get to hear the actor who portrayed "Data" speak; I could survive - there would always be next time.

About a week before the convention, my dad said that he had gotten someone to work for him so that he could take me to the convention. I could tell he didn't want to go, but he wanted me to have the opportunity.

The next Sunday, I woke up very excited. I only ate a small breakfast after church because my stomach was too knotted to eat my usual Sunday pancakes. As we sat at Bob's Big Boy overlooking Riverside Drive, the cool breeze was even exciting that morning. I was actually going to be able to go to a convention.

Now, I don't know why, but I wanted to wear my costume at the convention. I think I must have thought that was the thing to do; so slightly embarrassed, I asked my dad if he minded if I wore it. Looking back, I can tell you I had every right to be embarrassed: dressing up at a convention - what was I thinking? I was 13, and failed to realize that people judged you on your appearance.

"No problem," he said, supporting me in my *Star Trek* adventure.

We left at about 11:30 and headed over Beverly Glen into Beverly Hills. Finally arriving at the hotel, we walked into the huge room that had booths set up selling wares. It was a true Egyptian bazaar as portrayed in the *Indiana Jones* films, except instead of camels, urns, and jewelry, there were Klingons, props, and trading cards... and figurines, videos, costumes, and other *Star Trek* paraphernalia that spilled over the tables that were set up throughout the huge room. We were immersed in *Star Trek,* and it was all up for sale.

With $50 in birthday money, I immediately started comparing prices at the different booths. I analyzed items that I already owned to see what kind of price they held "at market," and to see what would be worth "investing in." Seeing one of my figures priced at $23 made me realize the significance of my purchases that day. We continued to peruse the aisles of *Star Trek,* walking the complex at least three times: I was not going to be taken by a salesman dressed as Captain Kirk.

I left that day with bumper stickers, new figures for my collection, trading cards, Romulan Ale, pins, pens, notepads, a watch, three posters, some more postcards, and a audio cassette of "Data" singing, all of which would be carefully sealed in a box when I got home. And in that box – actually boxes – is where it all is to this day. But I was a savvy shopper and "needed" all of it.

But shopping was only half of the day. Seeing the sights of the convention was a completely different experience. People came decked out in the most elaborate costumes. I had the excuse of being 13; these geeks were in there forties and had spent their summer building an exact replica of a Borg costume. Whole families came dressed up as Klingons, with a tiny Klingon baby. The poor baby had no choice – the parents forced it to dress up and accept the show. At least I had chosen, on my own volition, to dress as a *human* officer. I wonder if the child would grow up to reject *Star Trek* or just live with it as a way of life without an alternative. At least I later realized that I could be a fan of *Star Trek* without having to accept all of the extremities that some attached to being a fan. Some people at this convention took the experience to the farthest extreme… too far.

But the real reason I attended that convention was to get to hear the speaker. Data was my favorite character on the show, and so I thought Brent Spiner, the actor who played him, would be my favorite, too.

The audience waited 20 minutes for him, as he was late in arriving. When he finally came out and started speaking to the packed auditorium, I was elated. He gave a little speech about what it was like to be part of the institution that was *Star Trek*.

"I am sure you would love to hear me speak about the intricacies of my job, but let's get right to your questions," he said sarcastically.

All over the room, fans raised their hands and started asking questions about what it was like to be in make-up… what it was like to work with the cast… what it was like being part of an institution – all questions he had already addressed. One woman even brought her cell phone up to the stage so that her friend could "speak" with Data. I don't think she could care what Brent was about - for her, it was all about Data.

Being young, I wanted to know about the person who played the character that I liked, not about the character who was played by this person on the stage. I finally got the courage up to raise my hand. He eventually pointed to me.

"Um, yeah, I was wondering, how old are you?" My riveting question was out, and I awaited his profound answer.

"Well, how old are you?" he responded.

Taken aback, I replied, "I asked you first."

He went on to the next question without answering mine. What did I do wrong? Did I care about the person instead of the character? I guess. My dad looked at me and said, "Let me know when you're ready to go. We can stay as long as you want, but just tell me when you want to go." Well, Spiner's curt answer and avoidance of my question was enough for me.

"Yeah, I'm ready," I said and we got up and headed out of the auditorium back through the marketplace.

I was glad I went to the convention – I realized for the first time that some people consider themselves fans of *Star Trek*; I considered myself a fan of the concept and execution of a TV show.

I watched the show until it's final episode and still find it compelling to talk about with other fans, who turn out to be numerous. I stopped buying figures when they came out with the fifth series, which boasted the crewmembers in their shore leave outfits that they wore once… off camera. I had enough of the hype – I just wanted to sit back and enjoy the entertainment of it all.

People don't talk about how they like *Star Trek*. They might be trained not to, but I do. I like *Star Trek* – so does that make me different? Or does being different make me like it? I think the answer is different for everyone. (I just hope I'm different from the freaks who have plastic surgery to have their ears look like Spock's.)

TWENTY-THREE

I drove on along Wilshire, finally just blocks away from the Cell Store. It was just on the other side, the west side, of the congested 405. And just before the 405, the Los Angeles County Federal Building, as always, stood with a group protesting out in front. Just as the 405 is almost guaranteed to have traffic, so is the Federal Building almost always guaranteed to have a group out in front at the busiest intersection in LA. I always looked over, but never fully realized how their protesting made any difference.

Mr. Jackie, the once newspaper moderator, was also my senior year Advanced English teacher, and as a proud child of the Sixties, he tried to explain what protests meant to the class. Now, you have to realize his history: he was a lead singer in a band for a long time and an art and film student at USC. Who would've thought he'd end up a high school English teacher?

Mr. Jackie had a life of ups and downs and would frequently shared his "life-wisdom" with us. This was the term he applied to the lessons learned from the seemingly too frequent "down" experiences of his life. Everyday during class, he would assign journal topics that would usually result from one of these experiences: "Today," he would say in his raspy voice, "write about a time when you felt 'on top of the world.'" He would then go into a 15-minute story about how he was singing in a band, with a band, for a band, or near a band; and how great it felt until he got fired and was left "penniless on the street, alone without a dime to call home". He was always telling wild stories, claiming them to be actual occurrences. Sometimes, I think he was a good newspaperman because he was a good liar.

One day, he said to the class, "Aren't you guys a little upset? I mean, think about it: we used up all the fun in the Sixties! The Sixties used up all the fun. We had a purpose back then, sit-ins, protests, and marches. Now, you just go about your lives not realizing, not worrying." He over-dramatically paused and looked off into the distance, into his youth. And then, his daily directive: "Write about it."

And so with that feeble explanation: protests were *fun*? He had a point about my generation, though: when we were in high school, my friends and I often found that we *were* without a cause, without anything new and "fun." Back then, we could not fight for the end of a war or the release of a major international political prisoner. I felt like we even lacked a simple sense of community. No unity whatsoever.

Phil had the answer, though. On one of the Saturdays that I had driven up from San Diego, we were all hanging out at Dan's house in the Palisades. Dan was without a car, so we always had to meet there or else someone had to be his chauffeur around the city. We were just hanging out, searching the Internet for things to do, laughing, and talking.

"How 'bout a movie?" Nick asked. "I hear Val Kilmer's new movie is playing in Century City."

"No. No more Kilmer movies," Dan insisted, ironically showing slight annoyance at Nick's obsession with Val Kilmer since watching *The Saint*. Nick seemed to like to impersonate him more than he actually liked his acting.

"Besides," I said, "you know that when I am only up for the weekend – I don't want to spend it in a dark theater for two hours where we can't talk. Movies just aren't a good use of time for people who are able to have – and enjoy – conversations."

"Ah, come on Ben – don't be such a stinka." Dan feigned a New York accent. His voices and jokes were always on the verge of being annoying, but he was fun to be around anyway.

"Well, I'm not going to a movie. Sorry."

"Fine, what can we do then?" Nick found his way back into the conversation.

"Um, I could go for some ice cream," I said smiling.

"You and your weird obsession with ice cream. You and ice cream should go get a room," Dan offered and then laughed at his own joke. He always laughed at his own jokes, especially when no one else did. Then he'd ask why no one was laughing: "come on guys, it's funny. Oh, you just don't understand real humor."

"Hey, guys," Phil said, turning around from the computer ignoring Dan's comments, "it says here that there's a march today downtown calling for the end of sweat shops."

"So, there was a demonstration last Saturday for the ban of insoles in designer tennis shoes. What's your point? Someone is always protesting something." Nick had a point.

"Let's do it," Phil beamed. "Let's go protest!"

"What would we protest?" I asked skeptically, remembering Mr. Jackie's dismay with my generation.

Dan was quick to respond. "I think the question is: what could we not protest? Think of the possibilities." His eyes lit up in an insane-genius, Poe-ish way.

"I think I see what you are saying," said Nick. "But do you really want to join someone else's protest. It will take the limelight away from us." He had another one.

"There's always small groups protesting in front of the Federal Building in Westwood," Dan suggested.

I had kept quiet during their moment of revelry. I thought this might be on the verge of illegal, so I was hesitant. And Nick noticed.

"Uh-oh: Ben, what's going on in your head? Come on, this is a chance to exercise your freedom of speech."

"Yeah, " Dan chimed in. "Come on. It'll be great."

"I don't want to get arrested. I'm over 18, remember. You're all just infants compared to me. I'm old." I always felt so much older than these guys, even though both Phil and Nick were only a year younger.

"Come on, Ben. I am 18, too, now. And you're not gonna get arrested. We have the right to do this... as long as we don't disturb the peace," Nick persuaded me.

"Alright, but we have to protest something worthwhile," I conceded.

Dan suggested we end protest for animal rights, to which I responded: "You're the one who wears that lame leather jacket all the time!"

"I got it!" Phil announced triumphantly, again ignoring Dan and jumping from his seat. "Let's go."

So, we followed Phil out the door, and he drove us to the art store. During the car ride to get poster-making supplies, we discussed our slogans for our personal protest, refining them as we all talked at once.

We continued to create as we actually made the signs, too. Twice, Dan had a better idea than the one he had already started writing, so he had to use the back of two boards. We each ended up with two posters and a faint feeling of unity.

We again piled into Phil's Jeep, heading east down Wilshire to just past the beastly 405. We parked on a smaller street near Wilshire and Veteran and then walked to our position on the corner.

"This is gonna be great," Dan repeated himself.

"Okay," Phil said, " Let's do it."

We each took our signs and, almost at once, all held them up. Now, though we were unified in our protest, our causes were unique; we each called for solidarity but for different reasons. Phil held his sign the highest. "Bring down The Wall!" he shouted, quoting his sign.

Dan tried to out-protest Phil with his cried of "End Prohibition," but he lacked the energy Phil had.

Nick called out to passing motorists: "More Pope, Less Dope!"

And finally, trying to be safe, I was the farthest back. "Honk in support of Ice Cream," my poster read.

For almost two hours on Saturday afternoon, we stood at that intersection, united in protest. We shouted our slogans, shook our signs, and stole the attention of passing motorists. Our voices never grew tired or weak... at least during the first 20 minutes. We even attracted the attention of a homeless man who joined in with us yelling at motorists, though I am not quite sure what he was shouting.

About half way through the protest, we all switched to our second signs. By this time, I had come to the front of the group and was excited to hear a honk every now and again. When I switched signs, the new one read, "Cream of Broccoli is Murder."

Nick's new sign called for the release of a major political prisoner. "Free Mandela!" he shouted at the speeding cars, just a few years too late.

Dan's second sign – which was actually his fourth attempt – had a large dollar sign and simply read, "Reganomics," which he shouted firmly to the world.

Phil's idea to protest was not actually to lash out against the things we were shouting, but to protest the act of protesting. And for his second sign, Phil drew a huge red circle on his poster board. He had a diagonal line through the center of it, forming the international "NO" sign. This "NO" sign, though, had nothing inside the circle; it was just the red circle with a slash in it.

Phil resolutely held up his sign and, overpowering the

rest of us, shouted, "Stop it!"

Our protest probably made little difference for each cause, but I can safely say that the Sixties definitely did not use up all the fun. Sorry, Mr. Jackie.

TWENTY-FOUR

The Cell Store was on Wilshire at Bundy. I probably should have been cautious of a store that was called "Cell" – was the motivation only to sell, no matter what? And the fact that it was on Bundy didn't help matters, either. I never pass Bundy Drive without thinking a little harder. That exit off the 10 in Santa Monica has special meaning to me – and anyone who lived in LA in the '90s.

Since just after I graduated from eighth grade, OJ has been all over the news. Every station carried his slow speed chase live, setting the precedent for every other police chase, which is almost an everyday occurrence.

"Why do they always have to put this stuff on TV?" my mom questioned as she clicked off the TV.

"It sells," my dad replied frankly. I have to agree.

Since I had become aware of the news, it had been a never-ending cycle of overplayed, over-hyped dramas: Michael Jackson, Heidi Fleiss, Tonya and Nancy, Lorena and John Wayne, Amy and Joey – the list goes on. But OJ took it a step further on that Friday afternoon when he led the nation down the 10, adding to the already heavy Friday night congestion.

And so, the saga that was the OJ Trial began to consume LA. Bundy, Rockingham, Kato (both the man and the dog), Dream Team, and Ito all took on new meaning. The Trial only contributed to the myths that surrounded the smog and traffic of LA. But even longtime residents steeped in the reality of Los Angeles could not escape the celebrity of it all.

Erin and I had been hanging out a lot that summer – her mom would drive us everywhere in the leased convertible she bought when she turned 50. Without a doubt, Erin was my best friend. But she was also a faithful Simpson Murder Trial fan; she would just sit and watch the saga unfold. She'd call me up when a new "celebrity" would take the stand, whether it was a DNA expert or a housekeeper who needed a translator. She even bought into the gimmicks, buying the *OJ Legal Pad* and staying up late just to watch "The Dancing Ito's" on *The Tonight Show*.

When the trial coverage was interrupted or recessing, she'd beg her mom to drive by all of the people who had flocked to see the now-legendary Rockingham Estate or the infamous Bundy condo. I was in the car with her once, and that was enough for me.

We spent maybe two minutes in front of the Bundy condo because "No Stopping Anytime" signs were posted every few feet. This wasn't nearly as exciting as the almost thirty minutes we spent in front of the Rockingham Estate with assorted news crews and people who actually got out of their cars to look around, as if searching for evidence missed by the LAPD.

This was not the first time I'd been down Bundy since the fiasco that redefined the street. Once before, I'd been to the scene with Jason and his mom on the way back from a Santa Monica outing to get "the best coleslaw in LA."

"You've never seen it and the crowds that flock there?" Jason asked, as we drove along Sunset, towards the condo.

"Well, let's go add to that madness," his mom said, turning towards the salmon-colored complex.

We pulled up to see people everywhere and faithful news crews who continued to stake out the scene. Jason pointed out the window, indicating the tragedy that occurred behind the chain-linked fences.

"That's sad," I said. "I wonder how the people around here can actually live with all this chaos surrounding them."

Jason looked back at me and said, "Look. See, they use police like that to keep people from loitering."

I looked out the back window at the police car as he spoke. Almost immediately, the police lights flashed and Jason's mom swore. That $170 ticket was the reminder that the police were there to protect the people who stilled lived on Bundy, and that if you wanted to ogle at (or like) the media circus, you would have to park blocks away and walk to the spot. "No Stopping Anytime."

If these were my only two connections to the crime scene, I would be as connected as most people who lived in LA. But for me, my connections to the whole OJ saga went deeper. It went beyond the fact that Marcia Clarke was my aunt's neighbor. The connection was even more direct than my math teacher who had a friend who knew OJ and been inside the Rockingham Estate for parties. No, my connection was directly related to his trial, "The Trial of the Century." Or, should I say, "trials."

During my second year of stage crew, the second technical director came to run crew. He was a veteran of technical theater design and had all the skills necessary to "teach" us students how to produce a technically masterful production. My question was, with all his expertise and experience, why was he working in high school theater? To leave his legacy?

Unmarried with no children, he quickly found it necessary to tell us stories about his youth and his life. Now, if you are picturing an older, rickety man with failing health – you are dead wrong. Richard was maybe 37 years old, though he unsuccessfully acted and spoke as if he was as young as we were, which he definitely was not. He had a thick, indistinguishable accent that was definitely not from LA, and his dark hair was always a different shade of black. (I don't think he dyed it; I just don't think he washed it often.) Not very tall, yet very thin, Richard was of mixed heritage that constantly changed depending upon lighting in which he was standing; he was definitely multi-ethnic. For a man in his mid-thirties who worked in set construction, he was overwhelmingly frail.

He was a nice enough guy, but he always had a story that was a bit obscure but interesting at the same time. Later, when a group of us would reflect on his stories, we would laugh at the ridiculousness of them. I still remember one where he told us how his younger sister would lock him in their basement all night, but that he would be down there and just try to come up with a way to get her back. Another defining feature of his stories was that they had no real point.

He also had ways of giving instructions that were uniquely his own. He would sometimes treat us like children who knew nothing, giving us obviously basic instructions. Referring to the gaffing tape once, he yelled at our stage manager, "Listen up! This is red tape; this is yellow; and this, blue. You understand?" The next minute, he would mistake us for graduate students of technical theater; that same day, he would yell at all of us, assuming that we knew that a quarter inch saw had to be perpendicular to the square of the third side when building a two-wheeled cart. And other times, he would just make outrageous demands like "make the paint dry faster" or "You can't use the scaffolding; just hang those lights." He was unpredictably abrasive and unnecessarily annoying.

Frail, yet abrasive, a superior, yet annoying, he eventually lost all public support from the crew of students. During Brecht's *Caucasian Chalk Circle*, the crew found it difficult to work with Richard.

"I don't know how much longer I can put up with his crap," Dale, a three-year crew veteran, said.

"Well, at least you don't have him making you re-do your work because it isn't perfect. He forgets that this isn't our job like it is his – I do this for fun," Mike voiced. Mike was a senior who had also been on crew since the "good old days" when the guys on crew designed and built the set alone, only having a priest supervise so that an adult was around if something happened. "I don't know how long *I* can put up with it!"

At about this time, Richard was called for jury duty. "Maybe you'll get on the O.J. Civil Trial," I joked awkwardly.

"Who knows?" he said. One on one, when not talking about the task at hand, he was okay to talk to... sometimes.

Over the next couple of weeks, he came to crew fairly
regularly. When he started to come late and miss crew sessions,
I asked our Scenic Director, Fr. Hank, what Richard's deal was.

"Oh, he has jury duty," was his answer.

"Still?" I questioned, "It's been four weeks!"

"He got placed on a jury," he responded calmly as he
mixed a special color of paint with his finger.

"That's pretty cool. I wonder what it's for."

"Well, I wouldn't bother him about it. You're not
supposed to talk about a trial when you are on a jury. We're
lucky that he still gets to come and work with us. We would be
up a creek without him."

"You're right, I guess," I said as I walked back to the set
to apply a second coat of paint to a pile of futurist junk.

Apparently, I wasn't the only one who noticed Richard's
absences, and lacking the tact that most had, Cliff (another four-
year Crew veteran) asked him about it pointblank. "Are you on
the OJ Trial jury?"

"Now, y'all know I can't answer that or talk about what
case I am on," he said firmly – but not upset – in his muddled
accent. "Now get back to work."

Nothing more was said about it for the next week, but
before he arrived that next Wednesday, Fr. Hank sat us all down
and told us that we need to be respectful of Richard's situation
and not to make him feel uncomfortable. The snickering from
seats told me that the guys thought differently.

It went without saying, now, by "the talk," the secrecy,
and the length of his absence that he was definitely on The Trial.
We all knew not to talk about it around him or any of the other
adults, but in the car on the way home or while hanging out at
school, we always laughed about it.

"Think about it," Bryan said. "He could be determining
the fate of OJ. I wouldn't want him to determine my fate; I feel
bad for The Juice."

During Tech Week of that show, we'd go to school all
day and then stay in the theater until at least 11 p.m. every night.
It was like hell week for the football players, but no one cared

about our pain except our few fellow Crewmembers. This week was always a time of great energy after school, but lethargy during seemingly endless classes.

The dress rehearsal was the night before Opening Night, and Fr. Hank and some of us student painters were still putting final touches onto the set even during that last run-through. The crew was all there, too, dressed in their blacks for the scene changes; and since I was on the set painting, I was unable to keep them out of my "Prop Lair." Even though I had hidden all the really tempting props like guns and fake food (for some reason, fake food was as cool as guns to these guys), some of them still snuck in and played with things. Cliff, especially, liked to rummage through the collection to find something to amuse himself with for the evening.

"Oh, look at this," he said as he walked out of the "lair" holding his treasure.

"What did you take?" I confronted him as he turned the corner.

"Nothing, Grenaro. Calm down. It's just this." He held up a glove – a costume, not a prop – so I didn't stop him.

"What? Are you going to pretend you are Laverne or Shirley and watch it sail away on the beer-bottling conveyor belt?"

"Yeah, that's it. NO! Now go and paint; go do your painting thing. Don't worry about it. Leave my prize alone."

I knew Cliff was up to something but didn't care as long as he kept away from me. As I walked back to the set to finish painting in a giant mound of copper sand, I could hear Cliff telling someone, "Look, it's OJ's missing glove!"

During the first act of the show, I walked back to the "green" room (which was actually painted yellow), where the senior crew guys mostly hung out during run-throughs of the show. Cliff was there with Dan, who designed the lights for this show.

"Whatdaya think?" he asked me. "Is it a good prop?" He held up the black glove mockingly and proud.

"What did you do?" I asked. "Dip it in paint?"

"No, I delicately used red paint to make it look like it was done haphazardly. Artistic, eh?"

"It's cool," I agreed in order to abate any possible argument, playful or otherwise. "Just make sure Richard doesn't see it. You don't wanna get in trouble." I realized afterward that I was warning a senior about getting in trouble. What did he care? I left to make sure I was not associated with the malicious replica.

After intermission, I walked back to the "green" room, and on top of the piano, a true work of art caught my eye. Cliff's painted glove lounged there, holding an orange. The glove was placed in a way so that the inside revealed the word *Simpson*.

"It's Homer's," Cliff explained. "Matt Groening is my inspiration."

"What if Stein or Richard finds it?" I urged as if I was the one who was going to get in trouble.

"Ah – nobody's gonna see it."

I walked back to the shop to clean up some of the paintbrushes and the sink that we had used for the previous ten weeks. It took me a good 45 minutes to clean it all up, and when I walked back towards the stage, I poked my head inside the yellow green room to see what was happening. Apparently, Richard *had* walked in and found the art installation.

"No one touch anything!" he screamed. "I'm gonna call my bailiff and have this whole place fingerprinted. This is unacceptable. I can't believe it." Just before leaving he turned around and said, "No, better yet, I'm gonna get a rope and seal off the area myself. Don't touch anything. And y'all better have an alibi when I come back." He stormed out the other door towards the office, his rants carrying throughout the theater.

The group standing around was snickering. Even the House Manager, a religion teacher, thought it was a bit of an overreaction. I took a closer look and found that some additions had been made to the sculpture. A little white card folded in half stood up with "Ex. A" printed on it. The orange was still in the glove's grasp, but carved into the flesh of the fruit was the word "guilty."

131

"I didn't think he'd come in," Cliff explained to the small group, half sincerely, half sarcastically. "And honestly, we didn't know that he was on that jury for sure. He should've told us."

"Well, when the fingerprint results come back, it'll only show you, Cliff." I rubbed it in that he was going to get busted. "And aren't you 18 already?"

"Um, yeah, but you don't think he's really gonna call the bailiff?" He said overconfidently, trying to mask his over apparent fear. "And it wasn't just me: Mike carved the 'guilty.' So, his prints'll be there, too."

"Yeah, and, um, I did add the little exhibit sign," Scott, a freshman offered nervously. "I can't get in trouble for just putting a sign there, can I?"

I left them arguing and hypothesizing as I walked back to finish cleaning up the set. From that first day, I had a feeling he was on that jury, and his outrage at the crews' creativity proved it. I was actually impressed with the way the little vignette came out: the costume-turned-prop preformed as well as any actor could.

Richard left that night before the show was over; his bailiff never showed up, and no one got finger-printed. And he never returned to help "teach" us how to produce a set. The next day, Ms. Stein "talked" to the crew for 30 minutes about responsibility and the power in our hands. I wish I had the courage to tell her then what I told some of the guys afterward: "We don't have power in our hands, we have the power in our gloves!"

Later that month, on the day that the verdict came out, I called Adam and Bryan, almost hysterical with laughter. I was giddy at the sight of the frail man who answered the press's questions abrasively. Richard was there on the screen as one of the jurors who had found OJ responsible in the Civil Case. And he was clearly the most obnoxious one on the screen. So much for anonymity.

Richard came back infrequently in the next year to see what we were all up to. And since the trial had ended (and he was less on edge), he was more open about its effects. "Just last week, I was in a book store, and this girl came up to me and told me how familiar I looked to her. She asked where she knew me from, and I had to reply, 'well, I was on the Simpson Jury.' She nodded and agreed that she had seen me on TV." Even after his experience, his stories were still as stale as ever.

Everyone in LA was affected by the trial, some of us more so than others. When the verdict from that second trial was read, forcing OJ to pay all those millions to the families of the deceased, I felt a little bit awkward. Had the crew had a hand in the way the verdict came out for OJ? Nope, just a glove.

TWENTY-FIVE

My destination was in sight, literally only three or four blocks away. I was almost there. (*Almost* is the key here, though.)

As I approached Bundy, the golden gas pump light illuminated the dashboard. That pesky light is the visual equivalent to the beep of an alarm clock: no matter when I hear that beeping noise, even if it is in the middle of the day or on TV, it makes my heart race like I am pressed for time for something. I guess it's a Pavlovian reaction from years of hearing that sound as the start of my school day. Similarly, when I see that little gas pump light up, I feel the immediate urge to get gas and make the impish gold pump disappear.

I had been watching the gas gauge all day, hoping that it would last me. In freeway driving, when I can just drive at 65 or 70 for an hour, a quarter of a tank seems to last forever. But on the streets, with signals and pauses and rights of way given to pedestrians who make intimidating hand gestures at you, that quarter tank doesn't last long at all. I needed gas.

On my right, with easy access and reasonable prices, was a ARCO station. The price of the lowest grade was within a few pennies of the average I'd seen around the city, so I wasn't too hesitant about filling up there. I pulled in, turned off my engine, and prepared to pump.

I went inside the little shop and waited for the attendant to get off the phone. I explained that the machine wouldn't take my gas card. He then tried to run it on his machine inside, but it wouldn't work.

"Cash?" he asked in a word.

"I guess I have to." I opened up my wallet again to replace the card. I flipped to my bills and found that I only had three singles. I gave it to him but told him I would see if I had more in my car.

I started pumping the three dollars worth and went into the front seat to see if I had any money in the arm rest or ash tray (I tried to keep money there for times just like that – emergencies.) I found another dollar bill and almost four dollars in coins. I figured I could replace the emergency fund when I got home that night. I mean, how many emergencies could I possibly have in one day?

I carried in my handful of gas, and the man smiled as I turned to leave. I smiled, too. It's sort of funny how no one carries money with them these days.

As I was crossing back to my car, I turned and saw a sporty convertible Mercedes pull out of the gas station. I turned to finish pumping my gas but the gas wouldn't go. I looked up and saw that the attendant was not at his usual seat. He was standing in the doorway screaming at the Mercedes, which had now come to a stop about half a block away. I thought the car might have not paid for gas, but this was a "pay before you pump" station. Then, I heard a scraping sound as the silver convertible slowly backed up on busy Wilshire. A grating, rubbery sound came from the car, getting louder as it approached. As it pulled in, the car obviously had left the station without replacing the nozzle back on the pump. The whole hose had ripped from the pump and was being dragged across the asphalt. I started to laugh.

If that wasn't bizarre enough as it was, what made me laugh even more was that the woman who had ripped off the hose as she left in a hurry was the attendant's (the owner, I presume) wife. He was hollering at her, and she yelled back saying that she was rushed only because of the way he demanded her to do things. It turned into an argument about household chores, with the severed pump as a mere impetus for fighting over domestic responsibilities.

What's strange is that I found out that it's not uncommon for these pumps to be ripped off in a gas-pump rush. It's become so regular that the stations have a register key for the replacement fee. I think it costs just over $100 to replace the hose, and I heard that the rushed person has the option of keeping the hose, which I think would be worth the immense embarrassment and expense.

I don't buy into the idea that people in LA are always in a rush, though. Many people take their time as they change the radio, searching with dexterity for the best song on the dial as they speed down the freeway. We don't go plowing through intersections, blaring horns and narrowly missing pedestrians; and our pedestrians know that you never cross the street on the formerly "don't walk" signs which are now all flashing red hands.

For me, life moves fast enough without having to rush around. I like to be punctual, but not the point of cursing red lights, honking at upheld speed limits, and making my own lanes out of the shoulders, bike lanes, and sidewalks. But just because I don't actively pursue speed does not mean it's not a part of my life. Sure, I could've walked just a couple blocks down and taken care of my phone replacement, but I was stuck waiting for the attendant to start up the gas flow again.

TWENTY-SIX

I finally reached the small store; there was even an empty parking space right in front. I pulled right in, and as it was

Sunday, I reveled in ignoring the meter. Finally, I thought, things were going my way.

I picked up my now-wretched phone and went into the store. With no line, I went right to the counter and then recounted to the saleswoman what had happened. I was especially friendly because I knew it would get me farther than being upset about it. I mean, it wasn't her fault my cell was broken.

I explained everything and asked what could be done; and after smiling and nodding the whole time, she said, "You know what, my manager has to take care of this. He's at lunch – can you come back in, like, ten or 15 minutes?"

Great. I would have to re-tell the story and wait to do it, too. "No problem," I lied. There was no reason to get upset; that's retail for you. Again, it wasn't her fault the manager took a late lunch. I smiled and left, noting the time and figuring out how I could still make it to dinner.

I was sympathetic, too, because I had worked in retail for so long before college. After my dad sold his liquor store, he and my mom opened a gift store in the Sherman Oaks Mall (which, unlike the by-then defunct Galleria, was a partial set for the 90s film, *Mallrats*). For five years, I worked whenever I wasn't at school or home, transforming from child helper to store manager. By the time I left for college, I had worked closely with the employees, customers, and merchandise.

From my extensive retail experience, I realize that not all patrons have the consideration to treat employees with respect. I know the feeling of being talked down to because at 17, I was the one in charge. My parents left me to run the store in the mall: manage the employees, balance the receipts, deal with the customers. When a customer wanted to talk to the manager and I appeared, they seemed to think that I knew nothing and couldn't help them. Too often, customers, or the general public for that matter, make judgments because someone appears young. Age does not dictate capability.

We had employees that were in high school and some that were retired. One was a 72-year-old German actress who did commercials that aired in China. Another had worked with my parents from the time she was 17 and was now finishing her masters almost ten years later. One guy was studying to be a musician, quit twice, but kept coming back to work for us. We had quite a mix of backgrounds and personalities, and each had multiple strengths for our store.

Hiring and training employees comprised a large part of my managerial responsibilities. I interviewed many perspective employees, but could only offer positions to those that showed the most potential. I also conducted monthly employee trainings on sales techniques, new promotions, and policies. I was the store expert on selling techniques and customer relations.

And only after all those years of working with my parents could I understand how hard it is to work in retail. It's not a job I'd wish on anyone. So now, a conscientious retail employee has my sincerest respect... and sympathy.

After 15 minutes of stalling, roaming down the street, looking into the windows of clothing stores and boutiques, I returned to the little, out of place phone store. I thought, again, that I would finally be able to bring closure to an unanticipated day of driving. What can I say? I was a wishful thinker.

When the young manager returned from his *extended* lunch, I re-told my saga of cell phone destruction, not at all exaggerating the details. The manager looked at me with attentive eyes. I knew that attentiveness was gauged by his hourly wage, which couldn't be that high. I finished my story and waited for his reaction.

"Well," he said to me with a drawn out drone that was reminiscent of an 87-year-old. "Let's see." He started fumbling with the broken phone. "Yeah, we can replace it – you said you have the insurance plan on it, right?"

"Great. Yeah, I pay the extra couple dollars a month for insurance. So, do I just get the same one, or a newer model or what?" I was excited that things were finally working out.

"Sure. Sure. Just lemme have your last name and pull up your account." I spelled it for him three times. "Okay, Mr.

Grenaro, I just need your receipt, and we can have you out of here in two minutes."

"My receipt? I'm sure I have it – but not here; it's at home. Don't you have all the information you need off your computer system? Doesn't it tell you that I got the phone here and am paying for insurance monthly?"

"Yes, but to verify that the system is correct, we need the original sales receipt. It's a new policy. You understand, for your safety and protection." I needed a replacement phone, not side-impact airbags!

"Look, I don't even need a newer model, just any phone. I really need to have it with me." I'd grown dependent on having it, even though I didn't use it all the time. Cell phones are like a drug: you can resist and resist for a long time, but once you try it and see how good it feels to have a false sense power, it's hard to live without one. I'm not into drugs, but I'm practically positive I'm addicted to cellular. And besides, phones don't leave you with fewer brain cells after each usage… depending on who called you.

"You know what, I think I can do that – but the problem is, on transference of phones, it takes 24 hours if you don't have the original receipt. But I'll be more than happy to help you out if you want to come back tomorrow."

"Thanks for understanding and helping me out. Whatever you can do is fine, I guess." ("Retail employee," I kept reminding myself, "Retail employee.")

I guess could wait a day and pick it up after traffic died down in the evening. So all of Monday I'd be without a phone – no big deal. And he was going to give me the new model. I wasn't really happy, though.

I first got the phone so my mother could feel like she could always get in touch with me. She actually gave it to me as a Christmas gift so that she would have piece of mind while I was driving back and forth between LA and San Diego. But as soon as I got it, I became dependant – I'd be lost without it.

I hurriedly signed all the papers to transfer the phone number to the new phone and was off. The old phone was gone, so I was set to go. I thanked the two sales people again (for what, I'm not sure), and then headed out to my car. I heard Willie Nelson's "On the Road Again" in the back of my head as I started east to Pasadena.

TWENTY-SEVEN

My personal story in LA is not extreme; I didn't go from rags to riches like Norma Jean to Marilyn Monroe or Tom Bradley to Tom Bradley. I consider myself fortunate – not lucky – to be where I am today.

Sometimes, after meeting me for the first time and hearing just a little about me, people will tell me that I've done some interesting things. Thomas Edison did some "interesting things"; Ben Franklin did some "interesting things"; me – I just did my own thing.

I've heard people use *successful* to describe what I will be "someday," but what about now? And who says that what I've done even hints at making me "successful"? My mom does, but she's biased, too.

She's no June Cleaver or Carol Brady, but my mother can definitely handle herself. She has experienced a lot which has made her stronger, and I value her opinion, biased or not. Carolyn Ingalls would definitely be her TV counterpart, without all the horses and chickens.

As soon as she turned 50, my mother started swearing, and not just subtle, under her breath, "damns," either. She started really swearing with the best of them. I guess reaching the half-century mark means that expletives have the go-ahead. A guy's not really shocked until, in normal conversation, he hears his mother use the "F-word." I'll admit she's no George Carlin, but to hear profanity spew from my mother's mouth made me almost as uncomfortable as the time she tried to talk to me about sex. I'm not a stranger to swearing, and I've heard other women curse, too; but when my mother swears – it's over. She'd look at me and say, "What? You never heard the word *shit* before?"

So, my swearing mother thinks I am great; so does that substantiate my classification as a success? And do I care –*should* I care – if anyone but my mother thinks I am a success (even if she does swear)? Not really. Okay… maybe a little bit. I know I shouldn't, but I do. So, does that shape who I am and how I got here? I would be lying if I said no.

TWENTY-EIGHT

Pulling out of a parking space onto a busy street like Wilshire is almost as much of a challenge as trying to find one. As I sat there, waiting to start back towards the east, I stared into the stores along a stretch comparable to New York's overrated Fifth Avenue. It looked as though the cars would never stop coming, so I tried to read the sign hanging in the window of a men's boutique: "Be Yourself, Wear *Stylize*" (apparently the store's brand). The store was geared to a younger demographic: high school and college-aged, probably (and those that wish they were).

I would never shop in a place like that – it just wasn't my "style." But I bet you know the kind of guys that would shop only there, or J. Crew, or any of the other too-expensive-for-inferior-clothes-whose-label-costs-more-than-the-labor-to-make-it stores. As I get older, those kinds of "designer guys" seem to become fewer, but younger people seem consumed by their clothes.

See, in high school, *any* high school, people are identified strictly by how they look, how they dress. This was quite difficult to do at a school that imposed a dress code. Collared shirts only, no denim, and no sweat pants. No baggy pants or sagging, and absolutely no facial hair. No sandals, no hats, no chains, no logos, no vulgar language, no subtle inferences hidden within the lining of your new Tommy Hilfiger hi-performance, micro-fiber jacket. And shirts must always be tucked in.

For me, I never worried about the brand of my clothes: khakis from Sears and khakis from Banana Republic are still khakis. But others were known by their distinct clothes, or an item thereof. Jimmy wore one that one striped sweater; Brandon wore that blue zip-up jacket; Adam, his hat; Pete, his cargo shorts. No matter what someone wore, his clothes were who he was. This made a difference to some; others could care less. For me, I wore what was most comfortable. Clothes don't really make the man – the man makes the clothes.

In my junior year of high school, I was finally confident of my place in the broad cityscape. I was from the Valley, the center of my LA and the meeting place for my social gatherings. I began to actualize my unique ideas that some might say leaned towards unheard of, but could never be denied as fun or interesting.

One Thursday, for instance, I found my wardrobe to be limited because I hadn't had a chance to do a load of laundry that week. So, I took my only clean shirt, a beige cotton-blend from a sale at JC Penny's, and my last clean pair of khaki shorts, thus creating a coordinated outfit. It matched, though, in a peculiar way: both items were the same color.

Upon my arrival at school, I am sure no one really noticed me more than any other day. My friends had to have realized that I was wearing an oatmeal ensemble, but they didn't reveal any reaction of awe or disgust. I was definitely tame compared to the outrageous guys who would dress to draw attention to themselves with no real purpose (why would a guy wear a leisure suit on a weekly basis?).

To let them know, I announced to my friends, "Hey, it's Same-Color-Thursday!"

"Same-Color-Thursday?" Pete asked.

"Yeah. Every Thursday from now on, make sure all your clothes are the same color. Sort of like Rideshare-Thursday, but instead of alleviating traffic congestion, we'll alleviate color congestion." I wasn't completely convinced about my proposed remedy to the neglected problem of too many colors, but you must try to effect change, one step at a time.

"Um, yeah. You do that." He wasn't being mean, just honest. He wasn't going to participate; I could tell. But I told them all they should at least try it.

"It's going to be a new trend. Just watch." I smiled and headed off to another group of my friends to advertise the weekly fashion trend. I always wanted to be a trendsetter, and for the first time, I figured I was.

A week later, I came to school dressed in black shorts, a black Polo shirt, and, to top it off, black shoes with practically indistinguishable socks. I followed through; and even though I gave a reminder to all my friends the previous day, I was the only one who had. Pete still wore his long cargo shorts; Colin, his cords; and Brandon, his blue zip-up hooded sweatshirt. As I walked up to them noticing their multiple colors, I let them know that "Same-Color-Thursday will survive" and smiled as I passed without stopping.

The next Thursday, I was bold enough to be angelic. I wore white shorts and a white collared shirt and, of course, my white tennis shoes. And from the rest of them: nothing. The following Thursday: all blue (navy, not sky). This was the final color in which I had both matching shirts and shorts, so I knew I had to rotate the cycle and try not to wear the same set within a three-week period.

I kept it up every week, eager to see it catch on with at least one of my friends. They knew it was Same-Color-Thursday, they would say things mockingly like, "Have a great Same-Color-Thursday" or in class to a teacher, "How can you give a test on a beautiful Same-Color-Thursday like today?" They knew. It made me smile.

After six weeks, with great introspection and contemplation, I decided to wear my blue shirt and my khaki shorts. When I walked onto campus and approached my friends, they immediately noticed.

"Hey, what happened?"

"Yeah, today's Thursday, and you don't match." They were sincerely questioning why my clothes weren't coordinated.

I tried to explain as best I could: "Though outwardly, the latest trend has passed, it will continue to live on within each of us." They laughed and I laughed; and so ended the short-lived Same-Color-Thursday.

Very seldom, independence comes from conformity, and in attempting to be a trendsetter, I was as independent as I was when I chose to discontinue it. My job was to set Same-Color-Thursday in motion, not be its only patron. It would've continued on its own without its originator if it was meant to be successful.

Three years later, during my second year of college, I went up to LA to visit Jimmy while he was home from school. Out of the blue, during the middle of lunch, he asked my why I wasn't wearing an outfit of one color. "It's Thursday, isn't it? I thought by now, for sure you would have resurrected the trend." I hadn't thought about the days of "same-color" since it ended. And I guess it made more of an impression than I realized.

Sometimes, in the early morning darkness that is my life at 6 a.m., I try to figure out what to wear for the day. I'll pull out my black pants and a black shirt, and then I'll reject them. It's not Thursday.

TWENTY-NINE

As I turned my back to the Pacific Ocean, I knew I was driving less for leisure: I was now on destination drive. I turned off Wilshire towards Sunset Boulevard, traveling back on the road I had just traveled towards my destination of dinner. Just before approaching the foul 405, I passed the small retail center in Brentwood that was reflective of the area and its clientele: expensive.

Steve, a friend of mine from high school who lives in the hills of the Palisades, introduced me to the area when I got lost driving to his house. His dad had actually just opened a small café there called The Portobello Grill, and Steve assured me that I would find myself in the area more often because of it.

Mr. Duffy used to be a screenwriter, but found himself tired of spending long hours in front of a computer screen. "I could be watching TV if I wanted to stare at a screen. And no one wants you if you use a typewriter: you just can't keep up with these new, know-it-all kids coming out of Harvard."

His little place opens for lunch and dinner, and though I'm not personally a huge fan of his menu, it seems to do well.

He's always told me to stop by and chat if I was in the area. Stop by, I could do; chat – that was more of an undertaking than getting over the Sepulveda Pass. See, with Mr. Duffy, a chat turned into a conversation that was more of a discussion on the verge of a major debate. And there was no way to win that debate. I really did enjoy his company, and we spent many dinners, with Steve and Mrs. Duffy, discussing the finer points of whatever. What kept me coming back to the engrossing conversations was that Steve's parents, like my own, always encouraged me to do the things for which I had a passion.

When I explained to them that I'd joined the college television station and created a "Muppet-like puppet show," Mr. Duffy beamed. They seemed to be intrigued at the idea as I explained that it was a weekly half-hour show that starred a singing, pretentious broccoli and her ensemble of a carrot, an alien, and her nemesis ("the broccoli thief"). I did all the voices, and the show was basically unscripted, usually just parodying a well-known story or TV show.

While Steve and his mom were washing the ice cream dishes one evening, Mr. Duffy called me into his former study. On the walls were certificates of merit in writing and even an Academy Award Nomination plaque for a film from the '70s that I'd never heard of. He went over to the closet and pulled out a large trophy that I immediately recognized.

"Why do you have an Emmy in your closet?" I asked in

144

awe and confusion. If I had one, I'd think I'd keep on display.

"Read it," he commanded. I read through the slight tarnish and smiled largely.

"Wow, that's cool," I said, not knowing really how else to react. The inscription said it was for writing in a comedy or variety show and then had *"The Muppet Show"* printed in large letters.

"That's really impressive."

"Yeah, I picked it up at a garage sale about seven years ago for a mere 50 bucks." Some of the magic faded instantly, and more, as I drove back down to San Diego. I was still impressed at his skill as a writer; he could have been very successful in The Industry if he had stuck with it, but technology seemed to thwart him. I guess it goes to show you that anybody in LA can have an Emmy.

When I went to Portobello for the first time, I spent 20 minutes looking at all the décor, admiring the photos of stars and other LA celebrity memorabilia. In a dark corner just before the kitchen door, almost out of sight, was that Emmy. And just below it was a picture of Mr. Duffy, some other guys, and Jim Henson, each holding a statuette. He was quite a convincing storyteller.

THIRTY

As I passed over the 405, I saw exactly what I expected: brake lights in the dusky haze of the late afternoon. I thought I would take Old Sepulveda Road and avoid the traffic: no good, though – it was jammed, too. So, I was compelled to take Sunset through Bel-Air into the twilight. I hate it when I'm forced to take surface streets when I *need* to get to a destination by a certain time.

I really do enjoy driving LA's freeways: zipping from here to there in 20 minutes, across the city or to its outskirts. No place is too far, and if it is, it's worth the ride. No hassle of tolls; no lack of roadway. Freeways in LA set the standard for America and the world: true freedom and the pursuit of happiness.

And it's like that just about everywhere you can drive to in LA… except through the Sepulveda Pass. The 405 between the Valley and the Westside is the worst stretch of freeway. LAX and the Rose Bowl were equidistant from my house in the Valley, but it always took double or triple the time to get to LAX because of the Sepulveda Pass.

No matter what time of day or night I drive it, there is always braking, stopping, rubbernecking, and other unnecessary slowing justified by "there's always traffic in the Sepulveda Pass." Freeway Gods at work, more likely. I've resigned myself to taking other routes: either over the hill on Beverly Glen or a surface street that connects to the Hollywood Freeway. The 405 is a beast that devours actual travel and excretes traffic.

My dissatisfaction with this five-mile stretch of freeway has oozed into Westwood, too. The home of UCLA has put a bitter taste in my mouth. Maybe it's offensive, though, because UCLA rejected me (twice), a message that still resonates in my LA-born heart.

When looking to higher education, I only wanted to go to UCLA – no other college or university interested me. I toured the East Coast in search of "the college for me": Bates, Tufts, Amherst, and the like. Nothing – I felt no connection when I visited. The cold, snowy winters and isolation of Maine were not for me. I knew LA was the only place for me. *UCLA*.

After taking the SATs, I found myself eligible for more than I aspired to, but LA is where I wanted to be; I couldn't convince myself to change my mind. I couldn't even get myself to fill out the other applications I had gathered. And my mother had gathered. And my counselor had gathered.

What I couldn't gather was why everyone wanted me – and all my peers – to apply to at least *nine* colleges: three "shoe-ins", three "realistics", and three "long-shots". Only one for me, though; that's all I needed. My friends were each applying to 47 different colleges to "make sure" and "have options." I opted for no options. No options, no choices, no tough decisions.

When the UC Application arrived, I delicately filled out all the boxes: extracurricular activities, service activities, work experience. My academics were not bad; and true, my SAT scores were not as high as top applicants, but I only took the test once and without any prep courses.

My application essay, on the other hand, was another area of debate. I had difficulty putting words to paper and couldn't seem to talk about myself very effectively. When I am faced with a challenge, like writing the essay, I've always tried to be creative.

On my computer at home, I have the embarrassingly awkward, *what-was-I-thinking* drafts of my college essay. In one version, I wrote about my encounter with the OJ Trial as a "theatrical experience". In another draft, I was very metaphorical and spoke of a young, Roman peasant whose parents owned a papyrus store in the agora. Very creative – not good for a college essay, though. I spent late nights arguing with my parents about the essay; I was determined to do it my way.

"I guess there's not much else we can do but accept that. You have to make choices for yourself, now."

I looked back at them and responded, "*Now*? I have been making my own choices since I started this whole process, since I chose to go to St Vincent's, since chose to work for you. I'm going to do it my way."

The irritation of the whole application process manipulated my sense of self-worth. I was being judged on standards which I don't particularly believe are accurate, even though I can do well within those standards. I forged through it, though, to make my parents happy, making sure they knew I was doing it for that reason.

Just before I was about to seal my application's envelope – and my fate – my mother approached me with yet another suggestion: apply to at least one other UC school.

"Just in case something doesn't go exactly as planned,

you are going to want to have a back up."

I saw her logic and wanted to appease her, so I checked another box. Santa Barbara was too relaxed, Irvine was too technical, and Berkeley was, well, too "Berkeley." San Diego looked good, so I marked that box and wrote a check for 80 dollars instead of 40. One application, two schools – two for one. Not too bad.

Then, I waited… and waited… and waited. Everyone got their letters, and I, mine from UCSD – but no word from *my* school. I knew it would be coming… any day now… I just had to be patient… and wait… and listen as everyone around me was excited about getting into their first choices…. and then wait… and wait some more.

"Don't worry," my counselor, Mr. Herro, said, "it'll come. I am sure you got in." He tried to encourage me, but looking back, I realized its absurdity. What kind of counselor would suggest every school that I did not want to go to: a small school in the middle of Alaska, a recently turned co-ed school in Atlanta, and a school in the middle of the country surrounded by cornfields? My counselor. What I wanted was simple: LA.

After I'd found that most of my class was accepted (even Adam), the letter from UCLA finally arrived, and I was extra-confident of their answer. When I got home from stage crew that night, I excitedly, and without hesitance, opened the letter.

"I told you that you should have applied to more schools," Mr. Herro said the next day. "Now, you are left with only two options—"

"One," I said, dissatisfied. "I have only one option: San Diego."

"No. True you have that option, which is not a bad one. I went to school down there, you know. But then again, I am just a college counselor now," he joked about his occupation – if only knew what a joke it was. "You can also appeal your status at UCLA – you've got nothing to lose."

"Alright, yeah. I mean, if they're gonna reconsider

148

anyone, they should reconsider me. I'm the student they should want, not Adam or one of those other guys they let in," I was a little irritated that so many other people – who didn't work nearly as hard as I thought I did – got accepted. I was angry. "I should have been the one to get in."

I appealed because "UCLA was the only school" I wanted attend. More letters of support, more phone calls, more waiting. Mr. Herro knew the Director of Admissions there, so I thought that might help. Finally, another letter came to my house in the Valley, and my attitude changed.

"UCSD won't be that bad," I thought and told anyone who would listen. "But, boy, did UCLA make a mistake." I was convinced that admissions offices were not run efficiently and let the good applicants slip through their outstretched hands.

So, except for that one stretch of the 405, I still love to drive on LA's freeways. Sometimes, the greedy God of the 405 lets his paranormal pet run unleashed into all eight lanes, across both directions of traffic, and up the canyon walls. Its festering den, in a word: Westwood.

THIRTY-ONE

By now, I was tearing down the street, making decent time to get to Pasadena by 5 p.m. It should have only been another 30 minutes to get there – no big deal. I figure if you live in LA, you should be grateful you have the mobility to get in your car and go. In places like New York City or Washington, DC, the roads aren't really conducive for cross-town trips. After driving from the Valley to the South Bay, though, nowhere within the city is too far away.

The great network of Los Angeles connects a chain of people that spreads beyond the civic limits and throughout the nation and world. No matter where I go, I am connected with people who know someone I know in LA. And if a specific person does not connect us, there is a common link to a place or event in the city. The network never fails.

When I first got to college in San Diego, I looked for people with whom I had something in common. The first question and connection came with: "So, where are you from?" When "LA" was the answer, we could immediately share stories of the freeways and the excitement of living in our hometown – which was not a town like those from San Ansolmo who might claim to be from a "town." I admit it: I looked for the "LA" in a person.

After my first month of making of "friends" in college, I started finding my niches. Still, at that point, I didn't realize that my first impressions weren't so great. They would later tell me the same thing I had heard often, but only after time had passed.

"Ben, how come we're still friends?" Beth asked as she Sam, and I sat together at Souplantation during one of our personal college reunions. Beth and Sam were both from Palos Verdes and had gone to high school together. I met them both my first month of college, and we have been a strong trio of friends ever since. In fact, they are really the only college friends that I see and talk to regularly.

"Well, maybe because we're each persistent?" I said with a smile.

"I would've never guessed we would still be friends after our first encounter. Sam, I was ready to kill this little freshman who we now call a friend."

"No - Ben? I can't see it." Sam was overdramatic. Let's just say we all matured a lot after our first year of college. When I first met Beth during the first month of school, I was trying to convince her to sign up for the college TV station which I had so eagerly joined my first week of school. While passing her table in the dining hall, I merely suggested that she come to the meeting that evening. She said she had plans, but I was being "charming" and continued to pursue the subject. I later learned she finished her meal by throwing half of it away in order to leave the persistent freshman. When I walked into the meeting that night, she was already there. Apparently she had been a member of the group the year before and had just missed the first few meetings.

"Seriously, though, I think that we just had a lot in common."

"Yeah," agreed Sam. "We do seem to hit it off when we hang out, no matter who else is around. "

After that uncomfortable meeting, the TV station crew went for a late night snack at Denny's. I ended up sitting next to Beth, and we started talking and getting to know each other. (Remember, I never knew how annoyed she was until the next year.) We both had season passes to Disneyland, which made us friends, and when we found out we were both from LA, the deal was sealed.

I met Sam in a more conventional manner at a Residential Council meeting, and we immediately, without any uncomfortable annoyances, became friends. He was as active and involved as I was, and we had a similar sense of humor. Scott and I discovered that his mom was in the same social group as mine, the CIGS: Caring Individuals for Global Safety. (It was basically a glorified social club that had a fancy name and the same fundraiser each year.)

The three of us had a lot in common, but above all, we connected because we were from LA. My face lit up when Beth mentioned dinner at Ed Debevic's and Dodger Dogs in Dodger Stadium; she beamed when I explained I drove by the Hollywood Palace daily and often ate in Hermosa Beach; and Sam smirked when we spoke of the Lakers or driving the 110.

Without initially realizing that the two of them already knew each other, I had found my two favorite college friends. Somewhere along the line, the three of us started to hang out. But as school continued, we each became busier with our studies or other activities. We still hung out as a trio when we could, but not as regularly as when I had first arrived at the campus. But our friendship never faltered.

Though we three were friends equally, I felt more

connected to Beth. Who am I kidding – I was attracted to her for the first 6 months of knowing her. But as time passed and I learned about her past - her high school choir experiences, her boyfriend from Germany, her sister's obsession with Pogs, her parents' background at UCLA, and her recent breakup with her boyfriend from high school – I realized I needed her as a good friend instead of a girlfriend. (And that fact that she made it clear that she "could never date a person like" me cleared things up pretty well.) So, we were friends; I could handle that. So, I filled her in: she learned about my time on Stage Crew (with that crucial piece of citrus fruit), going to an all-boys school, my adventures with ice cream, my trip to Europe, and how I "knew retail." Just friends, though.

Because she claimed that everyone on the Peninsula knew everyone else, I revealed my list of PV contacts – she was right. She knew the guys that went to my high school and even my dad's cousins.

Beth and I had the Los Angeles connection, which we often discussed and laughed about, but we also were similar in things unsaid. She showed her beliefs and values indirectly through her actions and how she treated and spoke to others. She was a caring individual who was confident and held high standards for herself, and those around her. Even though her parents pushed her, she consciously did the best she could, not for them, but for herself. She was an independent thinker. And though she had a distinct way of reacting to things that upset her, that was Beth; I accept her for it. She obviously accepts me with all my quirks (though she doesn't quite understand my enjoyment of *Star Trek).*

During our first year of friendship, she would talk and say little revealing things about her life, allowing me to piece together a larger picture of her. I do that with most people, but with Beth, she wanted to be a closed book and would feign frustration when she recognized she had revealed another tidbit.

After that year, she learned well that I remembered little facts about people. Obscure little bits said in passing are the pieces of information I would hold onto. I knew all about her pre-college life by little things she would say in a moment of uncontrollable trust. But by this time, she knew she could trust me. And I truly trusted her.

Our conversations would often turn to the past in LA. I learned all about her high school friends. I told her about my experiences at St. Vincent's. But what was interesting was finally hearing the girl's side of a relationship. Coming from an all-boys school, we all discussed which girl had done us wrong by breaking our hearts; rarely had I heard the tales of woe from the female perspective, at least not a friend whose side I would take. She'd recount – in pieces – her break up with a guy who she thought she really loved. This especially peaked my interest. The whole concept of being in love while in high school – was that actually possible?

Hers was a two-year relationship that ended like a scene from *Beverly Hills, 90210*. He broke up with her; and then got back together with her; and then broke up with her again a week later. But what made it interesting from my perspective is that she was so hesitant to talk about any of it. I could tell it still hurt her: something would slip out, and she would catch herself with a painful look appearing in her eyes. Sometimes she would keep going, telling about plans they had made for their future together or times they had done something special. I learned all about this guy, and from what I gathered, he was a nice guy, like someone I'd be friends with; but I didn't like him because he truly hurt Beth.

The summer after we became friends, the two of us were both back home in LA. We talked about once a week, probing each other's activities to see if there was any connection to our respective pasts that we both knew about. She asked about Scott Bradley and Chris, both of whom she had met when the came to visit me. I'd ask if she ran into any of her ex-boyfriends.

"I think I saw his car, so I took a right into the Ralph's parking lot. I parked and ducked down. I didn't want him to see me, you know."

"Was it him, though?"

"I'm not sure, but better safe than sorry, right? I just don't

153

want to let him see me. If he's not going to make the effort, he's not going to be able to see me by chance, either." Over a year later, she was still mad that he didn't even want to stay friends after the breakup.

That summer, I started making the trips to see Sam and Beth in Palos Verdes, the ranch community that became the home to the wealthy and, more importantly, the home of my friends. At 9:30 at night, I would drive 45 minutes to make the 10:20 showing of the latest Mike Meyers movie at their theater in Torrance. They both came, with their siblings, to the Third Annual Ice Cream Party. Our summer brought a new aspect to our college friendship: LA. We moved beyond being just "school friends" into "home friends." I knew our friendship would last.

Beth, Sam, and I shared a bond that has developed from a trusted friendship and a common metropolis. Without this bond, who knows if we'd still be friends today.

THIRTY-TWO

I took Santa Monica Boulevard for a while, trying to have fun, but I was becoming more anxious as the time passed. So, I second-guessed myself and decided to take a right at Beverly Boulevard. I traveled past Cedar Sinai Medical Plaza and the intersection of Burns and Allen, out of Beverly Hills, and into the Fairfax District.

Just past La Brea and just before entering residential Hancock Park, a yellow light slowed me down just as I was finally gaining some ground. I slowed to stop, noticing to my left a shiny, new, silver Jaguar, laying in wait, ready to pounce as soon as the light turned green. Just sitting there, waiting for a green light, is what had changed my whole day just hours before. Pouncing on a green light does not always set you ahead of the crowd. Sometimes, the everyday things we do make the biggest difference; and sometimes, the uncommon, extraordinary things we do change us the least (but I don't find that very often to be the case).

Back in my senior year of high school, I decided to make my schedule as flexible, yet academically challenging, as possible. I took Advanced Biology, a two-period class, which was then followed by Advanced English and a required Moral Theology class. I had another year of honors math with Ms. Davis, and I signed up for a directed studies class that would prepare me to take the Advanced Psychology test. My schedule allowed me to enjoy my last semester at St. Vincent's.

During the directed studies class, I started working rather hard... well, at least that was my intention. I designed a plan for that one unstructured period that allowed me to learn and review all the information that would be on the Advanced Placement test in May. It was a great plan, in theory.

Pete and Chris also had directed studies at that time, and as the semester progressed, we played around more than we actually worked. We would talk and study and joke and laugh and have a great social hour. It made senior year, well, *senior year*.

Both Pete and Chris had become my friends early on in my St. Vincent's career. We all liked to joke around, and we would spend most of our time together laughing at something or someone. We'd go to lunch or hang out on the weekends, and usually do so in the Valley since Pete lived in Alhambra, and Chris, in Torrance – both about 30 minutes from my house. One time, we even tried to go to Disneyland together, but after driving for 20 minutes, Pete announced he had no money, and Chris and I combined could not cover him, too. So, we ended up in The City of Commerce at a McDonald's for three hours. We always had fun together no matter where we ended up.

But at school during our "directed studies" period, we really had a good time. One day, for instance, while we were online at the computers in the Library, we started doing obscure searches.

"Okay, look up Ms. Davis; see what you can find. She

155

seems like the type who'd have an email address," I suggested. Chris typed in her name, her AOL profile came up, and he started laughing.

"What?" Pete asked sitting at the console on the other side of me.

"It says here she likes crocheting and Arts & Crafts," Chris laughed again as he told us. All three of us started laughing and then impersonating her teaching math while crocheting and making Popsicle stick birdhouses to demonstrate an algebraic formula. The assistant librarian came in and warned us to keep it down or the librarian would come in.

"Aren't you supposed to be studying this period, anyway?" she asked, concerned yet still friendly. She was an older woman who reminded me of my grandmother, but with more energy.

"Theoretically, yes. But this is learning, too," I said. "It's cooperative learning."

"Okay. You boys just keep out of trouble."

"You're talking to three of the best seniors at St. Vincent's," I said and smiled. "We're not going to get in trouble. For one, I don't want to get in trouble, and two, just because we're not studying, why would they get mad at us? It's not like we are cheating or stealing SAT books or bringing fake guns to school."

"Oh, I know, I know; I'm just doing my job and giving you fair warning. I'm off to check in a new shipment of books. Be good, Ben." And she left.

"You think we could really get in trouble?" Pete asked.

"For just searching the World Wide Web? No."

"Yeah," chimed in Chris, "They'd have to be really looking to make examples of us to get mad at three, high-achieving seniors who are just using the resources of the school." He paused. "Hey, I wonder if Snoddy's on here?"

"Yeah," Pete laughed excitedly, "I wonder if he's in here. Lemme check."

Mr. Snodgrass, our Advanced History teacher from the year before who had been at St. Vincent's for over 30 years, was quirkiest teacher I had ever met. Besides his trademark bowtie and silver hair with matching moustache, he was famous for demanding to be called "Professor" even though he didn't have a Ph. D. But all the students' referred to him as Snoddy.

He tried to stay current with the trends of his students, though he still had a hard time understanding why we liked popular music. With a catch phrase for every historical incident or person of note, Snoddy would lecture a class discussion and never let the students have the last word on anything – in class or out. As proof, I was sent out of his class more than any other student, even if it was during a club meeting or office hours. I guess he didn't like competition.

"I got it," Chris called, "Yeah, here." He moved the mouse around and then made a few more keystrokes. "There's no profile here. But it does have his address and phone number."

"Cool," said Pete

"That's cool. Lemme see," I said, leaning over to Chris's computer screen. "Where's that located? Anaconda Street?"

"I think it's in Hancock Park somewhere, just a couple of blocks up from Larchmont. Yeah, there's a downtown shuttle bus that stops on the corner there."

"Hey, wouldn't it be great if we sent this to him?" I smiled as the words came out: "You know, send a note to his room and have his address right there in front of him." Chris beamed, too.

This wouldn't work for any teacher except Snoddy. Whenever a note came to his room, no matter to whom it was addressed, he would read it to make sure it was a real note.

"The reason," he explained in class the first week of school, "is that once, many years ago, a kid who was an Office TA sent a note to his buddy, and it read, 'If the B-52's can roam, so can you.' I happened to glance at it and see that it was fake note. Now, I trust no note."

"It'll be great," Pete agreed. "Just think of the look on his face when he sees his address.

"Yeah, but we can't just send his address. There has to be more." I stopped to think for a split-second and then, "I know!

We can say that 'there is a party at...' and then put his address. It'll be great!"

"But who in his class can we send it to?" Chris questioned. "And how can we get it there without one of us taking it?"

"Yeah, too bad; that was a pretty good idea, too," Pete said disappointedly.

"What are you talking about," I questioned, offended. "Of course it'll work. We can send it to Scott Bradley; he's in that class right now. I walked by last week and saw him in there. And as for sending it, we can get one of the TA's from the Student Center to send it. It'll work, and it'll be great. Come on."

"Okay," said Pete, "Here, look at this." While we had been talking, he had typed up the party flyer. "Does this look good?"

Chris and I both looked and laughed as we saw the party flyer with Snodgrass's address right there.

"Do you think we could get in trouble for this?" Pete asked concerned.

"Listen," I said, "were not going to get in trouble for this. I will even sign my name at the bottom so that he knows it's from me."

"Yeah, he's got a good sense of humor, " Chris said.

"And if anyone is going to get in trouble, it'll be me." I paused, then added: "But, if I do get in trouble, I'm taking you guys down with me." We all laughed; then, Chris stopped laughing.

"Wait, I didn't do anything. I just looked up the address," Chris defensively said. "You guys are the ones who did this." We stopped laughing for a moment, and then he added: "But don't worry, I don't think you could get in trouble for a little joke."

"Yeah," I agreed with a final chuckle. "Come on, let's go get a TA to deliver it." The three of us scurried from the library, note in hand, and went to the Student Center. Once there, I signed my name, laughed, put Scott's name on it, laughed again, and then gave it to a TA to take to Mr. Snodgrass's room...and we laughed some more. The three of us were giddy with the thought of our little joke.

The TA came back and said he delivered it and that nothing happened. We figured Snodgrass just threw it away or chuckled without any public reaction.

"See," I said, "no big deal. I'll ask him tomorrow what he thought of it."

I told a bunch of my friends who were taking a second year of "Professor" Snodgrass what we had done, and they cracked up. Everyone I told did, saying that it was a really slick joke. And the week ended without incident.

The following Monday, during my directed studies period, I was in the library with Pete and Chris as usual. I was working on an assignment for Ms. Davis's class, Pete was reading a book off the shelf, and Chris was reading *Hamlet* for English Class. The assistant librarian came over to me and said they wanted me in the main office.

"Oh, I wonder what for?" I said honestly. "Maybe they want me to do an errand or something. I'll be back, guys."

I walked over to the Main Office without a care until I started walking up the steps.

"Crap," I said under my breath. "I wonder if this about the note? Nah," I reassured myself it wasn't, but my heart wouldn't stop racing as my palms started to sweat. I hadn't seen Snoddy since the note was delivered, so never had a chance to check to see if he thought it was funny. "Oh, no." I thought.

I opened the office door and saw the three secretaries, my friends who I visited at every break and even between classes to enjoy the candy on their desks – candy I had started to supply because I was the one eating it all. I forced a smile and approached one of them, the admissions secretary, and said, "Yeah, someone wanted to see me?"

She kindly pointed and replied in a motherly tone, "You are gonna want to talk to Ms. Reyes."

I walked to the next desk: "Yeah, did you need me?" I was scared to death now. The ladies in the office were not being as informal as usual; I knew I was in for it.

"Please take a seat and Mr. Chestess will come and get you," she said professionally.

"Eeeeee," I said trying to relax myself after being called to the Vice-Principal's office and saying what everyone must have been thinking. "I guess I'm in for it." I smiled big, trying to maintain my composure, which I could feel slipping away from me. I was auditioning all over again, but this time, I couldn't opt out of it – no running to the prop room.

"Grenaro, come on in," he said, returning to his office.

I sat down opposite him and thought, this isn't going to be that bad. Then, he spoke, "Did you send a note Professor Snodgrass's class?" My heart was beating faster than I had ever felt it beat, faster than after the earthquake.

"Yes," I responded firmly. My teeth clenched, and I my breaths were short and deep.

"What were you thinking?" he raised his voice. My hands started to shake: I was not a fan of confrontation. "We're looking at suspension here."

"W-wait, what?" I said. "Wait, wait, wait a minute" I repeated, trying very unsuccessfully to regain composure as it slipped away faster than I could comprehend. I went from "Ben, High School Senior," to "Ben, 6-year-old who just spilled mustard all over his shirt that his Mother had warned him not to spill on" in less than 5 seconds.

He went on, I'm sure, reveling in the fact that he had "cracked" me without having to say very much. "You crossed the line. See," he drew an imaginary line on his desk. "Here's the line. You crossed it."

I was a wreck by this time, frantic that, in my last months of high school, I would be suspended. "I know, I thought it would be funny. Please," I begged incoherently. "I'll do whatever. I am sorry. I know it was wrong, but I thought it would be funny."

"Tell me who else was involved… and we're not going anywhere 'til you do," he threatened, as if he had to.

"No problem," I said cooperatively wiping my eyes, starting to regain some of my dignity, though very, very little of it. "It was me, and Pete, and Chris, and Gustavo. Chris looked up the address, Pete wrote the note, and I signed and sent it. And Gustavo delivered it. But we made him. I– He really didn't do anything." I was feeling better with every word I spoke, but I was still shaking with my heart on its 4000th lap around my chest cavity.

He said I could leave and go sit in the infirmary until I felt like I was ready to go back to class. I walked awkwardly and embarrassedly past my friends, the secretaries, to get to the infirmary.

And I had my punishment, and it was not suspension. Detention and an apology note to Snoddy – not too bad. I still maintained that what I did wasn't wrong, that it was just a joke and in good spirits, but I had to deal with an administration who understood that, but could not let it slide just because I was the infamous Ben Grenaro.

I'd never been in trouble before that day; my high school conduct record gleamed except for that incident. My detention, which the Jesuits aptly called JUG (Justice Under God), was for five days after school and then a member of the "elite" clean-up crew after the prom. The punishment wasn't too bad, in the grand scheme of things.

"You're a rat, you know," Mr. Herro, my counselor, said jokingly when I told him how it all happened. "It's a great joke, and I am sure you really got Snodgrass; but I can't believe you ratted everyone out."

"Hey, I told them going into this thing that we were all gonna go down together… in a blaze of glory, no less." I was able to joke about it after the initial shock of being called into the office. "So I crack under pressure; let that be my biggest flaw." We laughed about it for the rest of the school year.

Even other teachers, who had apparently heard about the joke in the teacher's lounge, congratulated me on getting Snodgrass.

"Nice one, Grenaro. Next time, though, don't get caught," said Mr. Brown, who had the reputation of being a prankster among the faculty.

Chris and Pete were upset at first that I named them so fast, but they got over it within a day or two. We'd become famous among those who were in Snodgrass's classes as the ones who had "gotten him." Pete got the same punishment as I did, and Chris was let off as an accomplice.

The thing is, I was planning on owning up to it, otherwise, why would I have signed my name on the note? I got Snoddy, and I could be proud of that. I was willing to take the punishment for that feeling of "gotcha." And on top of it all, while cleaning up after the prom, the Dean said we could take the unclaimed decorations; I got a life-size Nancy Sinatra poster, which I guess is cool, if you like Nancy Sinatra.

THIRTY-THREE

Speeding down Beverly, I turned left at the Wilshire Country Club onto Rossmore, which subsequently turns into Vine Street about two blocks later. Heading towards Hollywood, with its sign in the distance, I knew I was going to be later to dinner than I had thought. I figured I'd take Vine to Franklin, then over Los Feliz Boulevard to the 5 or the 2. So, up Vine I drove with the Hollywood Sign as my North Star.

Vine is one of my favorite streets in LA. Not very long, you can travel its length in about 10 minutes. Passing Melrose and Santa Monica, the Dolittle Theater and the old, burnt out TAV Theater (where they filmed Chuck Woolery's classic, *The Love Connection*), an Army Surplus store and the Hollywood DMV, Vine has everything one could need. And when it crosses Hollywood Boulevard, the street is the epitome of Los Angeles's entertainment capital: the Capitol Records building, the Walk of Fame, and somewhere within the vicinity, a billboard of Angelyne, LA's self-proclaimed billboard goddess.

But what really captures my attention as I drive down Vine is the Catholic Church. Our Lady of the Blessed Sacrament is one of the most ornate and detailed churches I've seen. From St. Peter's in Rome to the "bishop's hat cathedral" in San Francisco to the nation's first cathedral in Baltimore – I've seen some magnificent churches. But this building holds more than just weekly masses.

In my 13 years of Catholic schooling, I have come to learn that the church is not the building, but the people who come to worship in it. Blessed Sacrament is a special church for that reason. Now, this isn't the metropolis's Catholic Cathedral, that's downtown and run by the cardinal. No, Blessed Sacrament is a Jesuit Church, run by the group of priests that run Loyola Marymount University and my high school.

To understand the importance of this church, you must understand that Jesuits seem to be Hollywood's favorite Catholic actors. Sr. Mary Henry told me that Franciscans and Dominicans tried, but the Jesuits seemed to have the training to perform. Maybe it's part of their preparations for the priesthood. At St. Vincent's, one of the younger priests told a group at a retreat that his "Director of Priestly Training," who has since become a bishop who assists the cardinal in LA, would offer classes in comedy so that new priests would "not be too boring." I'm not sure if that was a change that came from the *Vatican II* council in the '60s, but it would have been great if they had that philosophy when some of the older priests were trained. So, apparently, the Jesuits at Blessed Sacrament are prepared for Allen Funt at anytime.

And it's a good thing, too, because that church and its clergy have been used in more TV shows and movies than I can remember. Even my one television experience, when I was that extra on *Beverly Hills, 90210*, the church used for the scene was none other than Hollywood's Blessed Sacrament. Sure, the producers wanted you to believe that it was a church in Beverly Hills, but why film in "out-of-the-way" Beverly Hills – the church on Vine has so much more... character.

You know, sometimes I think I know too much about or have too much interest in religion and the church. I try to understand the beliefs of my faith, and question that which I don't understand. There are even a few priests who I had befriended while at St. Vincent's who I still question on Catholic issues. They're all great people, but very unique. Not just anyone can be a priest.

The people who join an order or study to even be a minister are special people, and they are a kind of person that has become rare to find in the 21st century. And it's almost cult-ish in the way that the ordained work and want to recruit new priests. Who can blame them? Would you want to hang around with the same, boring 90-year-old who is still convinced that the liturgy will return to Latin and talks about how "when he's pope, things'll be different"?

Being friends with priests, and not yet married, they seem to think I'd be perfect to "join up." Sometimes, though, I feel like a "kick me" sign is taped to my back, just out of reach for me to remove it. But it doesn't say, "kick me," though; instead, it says, "Ask me to be a priest!" I know it sounds absurd, but I think it's true – it's got to be. Why else would people continue to suggest that I become a priest? You know, you can be a person who cares for his fellow human being yet not have to be ordained.

My many years of Catholic school shouldn't make a difference - they didn't tell all the mothers that their sons should be religious or join the priesthood. In second grade, my teacher told my mother, "oh, he's going to be religious." She never said that about my older brother whom she had in class three years before me; and he was even more kind and caring than I was. What did I do to deserve such recognition?

Now, one of my elementary school classmates proclaimed for two years that *he* was going to be the next Pope. Yes, the next *Pope*. He didn't quite realize, I think, what that meant while in the second and third grade; but nevertheless, he promoted his papacy and wanted to be called Pope Michael. I thought it was cool, and at the time, I failed understand why no adult said, "oh, yes – he's going to be a priest" like they did to me. In more recent years, I understand why it would not have worked out: Mike is not going to be a priest. He enjoyed college life a little too much to take those vows.

And, I wasn't particularly pious in elementary school either. Sure, I was an altar boy, but over half the junior high was. My parents forced me to be at church every Sunday, so at least when I was serving, it made the time pass more quickly (but I still didn't particularly like it). Besides, all alter servers are fledgling pyromaniacs. I'm not sure why the Church trusts kids to light candles while wearing robes: it was a holy inferno waiting to happen. Sean lost his eyebrows one Sunday, and robes kept losing sleeves. So, being an alter boy, in my opinion, doesn't make you priest-worthy.

I think going to Jesuit high school might have perpetuated the priest-asking episodes. I was taught by about 50% laity and 50% clergy. The priests would always plug the priesthood as a "good choice to serve others." Sadly, they seemed to conveniently omit the part of the speech that said it was just *one* of the ways to serve your community.

And because I befriended them, the priestly onslaught continues. In no way do any of the priests that I know fit a mold, but they all seem to have the same script for recruiting: "So, have you ever thought about 'joining up?'" From Sacramento to Berkeley to Santa Clara to LA, they all ask. I guess "recruiter" is one of the job descriptions, along with professional mourner (it's no coincidence they dress in black) and social drinker.

And the thing that really irks me is that it's not just the Catholics. My Orthodox friends think I'd make a great priest – even some of my relatives. And since those priests can get married, they say I have no excuses. Um, hello? I'm not Orthodox.

And the suggestions really haven't ever stopped, though it has become infrequent since I started dating more seriously. Not two months ago, though, one of my former teachers who was just recently ordained asked me – no, he *let me know* – about the priestly opportunity in my future.

"You know, the Jesuits could always use another good priest," he said as we walked to our cars.

"Thanks for the info," I replied, "I'll keep that in mind."

He chuckled back at me as he got into his car. As he rolled down his windows, he went on, "I just thought you might want to know."

I walked up to his window to rebut. "Thanks, again, for the info. Some people have such a calling. But for me, I screen all calls, and that one went straight to the machine. And I don't think I'll be checking my messages anytime soon. But, thanks." I smiled largely.

I knew he was not offended, as we had bantered on the subject before, as I had done with many an offer of ordination. I still wondered, though, as I walked to my car, why this issue kept surfacing in front of me. God knows I don't go looking for it.

THIRTY-FOUR

After Sundays, Fridays are the best days to be in LA... and the worst. Fridays are obviously the worst because of traffic. But as long as you budget time for traffic that will start earlier, be heavier, and last longer than on other day, it's no big deal.

Fortunately for me, my high school let us out early on Fridays, which was the main reason why it ranks so high for me. It was the start of the weekend, and usually, a group of us went to lunch or to one guy's house right after school. But sometimes, when the sun was shining and the level of humidity was at its usual non-existence, I had the urge to do something different.

One such day, I found myself driving Adam home from school, as often was the case. We raced north to the Valley, taking that same route of Vine to Franklin Avenue. The usual course of action would take us from Franklin to Cahuenga to Barham and down into Burbank. Following a morning of crisp wind, the city's smog had been blown to the east and the Hollywood Hills rose before us, appearing to be close enough for us to reach out and touch the Hollywood Sign. When we reached Hollywood Boulevard, I asked Adam if he had any pressing issues he had to get to.

"Nope. Why, whadya have in mind?"

"Well, I've lived in LA my whole life. And everyday for the past three years, we've driven home from school and past these mountains. I've always wanted to see how close I can get to the *elusive* Hollywood Sign. You wanna try it?"

"Yeah, let's do it." Adam was eager to go along with my adventures, anyone's adventures.

So, we took a right (instead of a left) onto Franklin and then took a left again at Beachwood Canyon. Now, I had no map and no idea where I was headed except up to the top of the range to the massive sign. My only directional instinct was based on a fifth graded trip I had taken to The Griffith Observatory in Griffith Park. The guide had told us that the Observatory was actually built on Mount Hollywood and that the world-famous sign was actually located on the not-so-famous Mount Lee.

I knew there had to be a way to reach The Sign legally, without jumping through yards and dodging guard dogs. I had committed to memory a scene from *Entertainment Tonight* in which Mary Hart introduced a segment about the famous locations at which famous stars would walk their famous dogs in famous LA. One such location was on the trails beneath The Sign. They had to have a way of getting there, and I was going to find it.

With the windows down, we started up the streets that looked vaguely unfamiliar. Up one, down another, they wound around each other leading us back to where we began, but from another direction. The confusing streets would not tell the direct way to reach the top; the maze of intersections spoke in tongues that seemed to be purposely misleading.

"This is hopeless, Ben."

"Maybe, but since we've come this far – you know, eliminating the roads that lead nowhere – we should keep trying. Don't you think?"

"Oh, yeah. I didn't want to give up yet; I am just saying

it's discouraging. I guess that's why no one hangs out at The Sign." So we persisted, continuing through the hidden neighborhoods of the Hollywood Hills.

After just a couple more minutes, I got gutsy.

"Hey, Adam, I think I'm just going to ask someone. You know, see if they can point us in the right direction."

We were on a fairly level street for the hilly area we were exploring, so there were small lawns in front of the homes that lined it. An older woman, who looked at least 75, was in her yard busily doing nothing. Her modest house looked as though it had been there as long as she but had aged much better.

I slowed the car and called out my window an "excuse me." The woman looked over and stared.

"Um, I was wondering if you could possibly tell us the way to get to the trail that leads under the Hollywood Sign."

From her reaction, you think I tried to tell her she was a fat fool with triangles for legs and that she was going to have a circus in her yard from that day forward.

"YOU PEOPLE!" she shouted exasperatedly. She then turned and huffed onto her small porch, ranting about being bothered all the time and that "you tourists" were ruining her life. She turned and said that this was the last straw. I tried to defend myself, but she continued to shriek about complaining to the city. "Every time someone comes up this way, they want to know how to get to the sign. I wish they wouldn't even be able to get this far."

I discretely started rolling away as she continued to complain. I'd never seen someone get so upset about directions. You'd think she thought it was her private area that we were invading.

"Jeez, what's her problem?" I said out loud to myself more than Adam.

"I know. She could have just said she didn't know."

"Maybe she thought she was scaring us off or something? Was she wrong!" I drove on grinning with newfound determination.

We continued up the hill, this time via another street.

The Sign appeared to be growing as we came upon it. This street was residential, with most of the houses concealed behind huge shrubs or fences. We reached the cul-de-sac at the top of the hill, the closest point to The Sign we reached that day, and I stopped the car.

"Come on," I said, feeling more adventurous as the destination seemed within reach.

I opened my door and walked over to a chain-link fence but could go no further. We stood just below and about 20 yards to the east of one of the definitive symbols of Los Angeles and the West Coast. I stood next to Adam, awed at the point we had reached. I looked back and forth between The Sign and the city.

"I guess only the biggest stars and movie executives have 'all-access' passes to The Hollywood Sign."

"We could still jump this fence," Adam suggested, eager to break the rules. "No one is around."

"Nah." I was content with being dwarfed by the size of The Sign and its kingdom below. I was still within reach of the actual top, but it was enough for me to stand at a slight distance, outside of the splatter range of suicidal actors who failed to be shining stars. That was the story, you know: failed careers in the early part of the century resulted in climbs to the top of Mount Lee - and then, The Sign - to plummet into the city that caused failure. I was very happy to be on the other side of the fence.

"You ready?" I asked as I turned towards the car.

"Yeah, I guess."

We headed back down the mazelike streets and then over to the Valley. We stopped at In-N-Out and were still home by 3 p.m., just barely missing the traffic.

I left Adam that afternoon and headed home, only to be called back to his end of the Valley that evening. His parents were having some friends over for dinner, and he wanted to know if I wanted to come, too.

When I arrived at about 7 p.m., the Ginns were sitting out by their pool with their company. Adam introduced me to the other couple, a city councilman and his wife. When dinner was ready, we all sat together. The councilman asked us about school and where we were looking at going to college. I, in turn, asked him how it was to work for the city. He said he liked it, then, made an unfunny joke about voting for him next election.

"The best part is hearing from the people and really representing their interests. That's why I got into politics. Take today. Just before leaving city hall, we got a call in the office from an upset citizen." He proceeded to explain that the woman would talk to no one but him, so he took the call. He said that she complained that the city was becoming unsafe and that she was accosted by two youths in front of her home that very afternoon.

"She was calling from the Hollywood Hills – some old money there – and her complaint was valid. You see, the city has to act quickly before the residents of the Hills start unifying and making a big scene for *Access Hollywood* to report on. She said she was going to get all the neighbors to start writing letters not to the council, but to all the major news shows telling them that the Hollywood Sign was unsafe for the residents.

"All it takes is a resident or two to call over to one of the entertainment shows, and the city looks bad. Our office would like to avoid that, at all costs. So, we'll put up some signs or something to deter tourists. That'll make them happy, I'm sure. And it won't really take much effort or money – everybody's happy."

Adam and I discretely exchanged looks, and then I said, masking our true reactions, "That *is* interesting." It took all my energy not to grin widely at the knowledge that, perhaps, that woman who called her representative was the same one who we politely asked for directions that afternoon. The conversation quickly changed to the lighter subject of the last aired episode of *The Fresh Prince of Bel-Air*.

I offered to help clear the table, but Adam quickly said we were going to watch a movie inside – he didn't like to help clean up. We watched *Get Shorty*, and then I went home, having a great day of Hollywood adventure – and I successfully avoided traffic. It was a good Friday.

THIRTY-FIVE

As I approached Franklin, KFWB announced heavy traffic on the 5 and the 2 due to end of the two o'clock Dodger game. I'd rather not sit in traffic as I drove out to Pasadena, so I decided to take Barham north over into Burbank like I had done so often to get Adam's house. The 134 East was just blocks away from his house.

So, I took a left instead of a right on Franklin, but not without noticing the caution-yellow sign that clearly states "No access to the Hollywood Sign." These obnoxious signs adorn the entrance to every street that heads into the hills from Franklin Avenue and are new since the day I went in search of The Sign. We had to find out, on our own, whether it was possible or not to reach the heights of Hollywood.

Now, as it parallels the 101 Freeway on the east side of the Cahuenga Pass, Cahuenga Boulevard. merges into one northbound lane. Passing The Hollywood Bowl, The John Anson Ford Theater, and a number of cars, I sped up to overtake one last car before the lane reduction.

Defeated at the last moment, I had to remain behind a slow-moving, dirty mustard hatchback. I couldn't see the driver because the rear windows were obscured with bags and boxes. Crammed into the car and covering almost every window, the junk made me wonder if the car was driving or being driven.

As we moseyed along, I figured I could just pass the car at a point where road widens even though it's still just one lane. Just as I was about to speed up and pass the yellow storage unit, it took off – leaving the rest of us in a suffocating, black cloud of exhaust. I could finally go the speed I wanted to for the next couple of minutes as I squeezed between the speeding freeway and the sliced hill.

By now, the setting sun had cast a shadow onto the surrounding hills, accentuating the orange sky. Against this picturesque landscape, my thoughts flew faster than the posted speed limit. Intrigued by the exposed rocks on the hillside, I couldn't help but think of the destruction an earthquake would cause, crumbling the hills beside me and the freeway. The combination of cars and quakes and crumbling hills are such calming thoughts at dusk.

Earthquakes are nothing to fear, and I know I can survive them. It's just the potential damage to the people, not infrastructure, that tightens my stomach. If the freeway were to be damaged in this small canyon, or its cross-town cousin, the Sepulveda Pass, the city wouldn't come to a screeching halt just because of a severed artery – people would find a way and fight the re-directed traffic. But even with earthquake codes and retrofitting ordinances, the city is by no means earthquake proof.

The January 1994 Northridge Earthquake jolted me awake during one of the most vivid dreams I'd ever had. I dreamt I was standing on a ledge looking out over a vast, gray concrete emptiness with towering, yellow, geometric shapes obscuring the landscape. The gray shone in contrast to the yellow, almost a gleaming white. I heard muffled shouting coming from beneath one of the up-shooting pyramids, and then, I found myself pushing this huge, ornamental behemoth to reveal a hidden cavity. As the shouting got louder, the placid gray environment was cracking and crumbling between the emerging, yellow formation.

I was immediately thrown from my bed and knew we were having "The Big One." Everything in my room was in a pile on the floor; everything in our kitchen was in a pile on the floor; and huddled in the bedroom doorways, my family was like a pile on the floor. Riding out the aftershocks in the darkness of morning, we prayed for the unknown – did anyone else survive? The most frightening thing I've ever experienced was not the jolt awake, but the two hours afterward, living in isolation as the quaking lingered. What would daybreak bring?

Fortunately, my family was safe and unhurt. The chimney had collapsed, as had many others throughout the Valley. Just a few blocks away, along Moorpark Street next to the LA River, whole neighborhoods of apartment buildings had been shaken from their foundations; though not completely destroyed, they were definitely ruined. My school, a brick building, lost half a tile roof, and an auto body shop by the freeway looked like it just tipped over, the walls looking like they were still intact, just flattened to the right. And in the hills, one of the new, stilted homes, which was supported by beams on the hillside and overlooked the Valley, slid down the mountain into a natural ravine. That got a lot of airtime on the news, the splintered beams used as the background for their "Earthquake Strikes" title graphics.

Our real devastation came, though, not from the "earthquake goulash" made from everything that fell from the refrigerator and cabinets onto our kitchen floor, but from the carnage of merchandise floating in a pool of murky water at our family's store. The intense shaking split a water pipe above the ceiling and filled the store with a foot of water, but only after it politely knocked every shelf and all inventory onto the hardwood floor. Fortunately, the windows were blown out onto the street, so no spotting was evident from the indoor downpour. Those 15 short seconds of intense shaking closed the store for over six months.

About a year later, though the scars were still visible, the Valley had recovered. As Student Body President of my elementary school at the time, I had helped to organize and execute a drive that replaced items for the kids whose apartments had had to be evacuated. We even raised money by printing and selling a small booklet with children's suggestions for earthquake preparation and survival. As for the house that slid down the hill, it was someone's summer home, so no one was there to be injured. To this day, that lot sits empty, a reminder of nature's power of the "invincible" of LA.

Sadly, CalTech hasn't been able to perfect the art of prediction; earthquakes can strike at anytime and almost anywhere in California. Even though one can try to be prepared, there's really no way to be ready for it. LA will sometimes shake you down when you least expect it, which can throw you off balance, even if you are prepared.

When I hear a rumble, that instantaneous warning of impending vibrations, I tense up, only to be relieved when nothing comes of it. And if something were to follow, I'd be ready. After living through an earthquake, LA is nothing to fear.

THIRTY-SIX

With Universal Studios just ahead of me, I took a right down Barham as it turns into the Valley. Tearing down the hill, yet trying to stay close to the speed limit to avoid getting pulled over, I sped into Burbank, which could be easily confused with its neighboring Studio City.

Burbank is home to Warner Brothers, NBC, and Disney, among other major studios. Crossing over the concrete LA River and officially entering the City of Burbank, a driver is immediately dwarfed by the towering canyon walls of Warner Brothers Studios. Formerly the Burbank Studios, this facility films some of TV's most popular shows. All of their current hits and hopefuls have huge posters dangling from the wall as advertisements verging on bragging (maybe that's why my parents hung banners in their store window upon my birth). Whenever I pass that main gate, though, I'm always reminded of one of the final scenes in Mel Brooks's *Blazing Saddles* when his western movie passes into the reality of movie making with a horde of costumed actors pouring out of the main gate onto Barham.

Once I got my license, I was able to start running deliveries for my parents' store. Making the work truly exciting, most of those deliveries were to the studios around the city. Driving onto the Warner lot, I went into buildings that housed the creative minds that developed shows like *ER* and *Friends*. Though not floored by celebrities, I still find it interesting to walk by an open sound stage door and peak in on an empty set.

You have to be careful while driving around studio backlots, though. Universal, for example, has the roaming threat of a touring tram. Camera-armed tourists snap shots of anything around the huge soundstages that looks even vaguely "behind the scenes." While carrying the holiday deliveries to the Art Department (after parking just steps from *Murder, She Wrote's* Cabot Cove and the *Jaws* lagoon), a group on a tram snapped pictures of me as I walked from the car with the packages in my arm. Why they were so excited, I'm not sure; but maybe it was because I was still wearing my sunglasses and I waved as they passed. If you play the part, tourists will trust you in it.

One busy delivery day, I drove to Disney, Fox, Sony, Paramount, and the CBS Radford studios. Trips across the city to the different lots gave me an opportunity to meet industry executives, talent agents, personal assistants, and accidentally, a star himself.

That day of deliveries started at 9 a.m., ending about eight hours later. After lunch, though, I drove the delivery van over to the Radford Studios owned by CBS. Familiar with their outdoor sets, I was excited to deliver inside the surrounding buildings. One of the smaller studio lots, Radford was simple to get around, and my delivery was quick and hassle-free.

As I was walking back to my car in a visitor parking space, I had to cross the "major street" on the lot. I was three steps from the curb when a car tore from around the corner, just barley missing me. The car braked and from a barely rolled down window, I heard a familiar man's voice.

"Hey, you alright there? Be careful, would you!"

I said was fine, and the car sped off. I wasn't sure how I knew the voice until I glanced at the shrinking license plate: "SEINFLD."

I should have known who it was; they filmed his show right there on the lot. When I got back to work late that night and told my dad what happened, he didn't seem too bothered by it.

"But I was almost killed by a mega star!" I argued.

He told me not to worry about it and then, "I guess what

goes around, comes around."

"What's that supposed to mean? I never did anything to him – I may not have watched his show religiously, but that's nothing to hit a person for."

"Well, it may not have been what *you* did." He smiled. "See, a couple of weeks ago, I had just a one basket delivery to make, so I took it over there myself. As I was leaving, I could see a man was crossing the street up ahead. He was almost to the edge, so I didn't think anything of it and continued at my speed. Apparently, he had dropped something or stopped to pick something up and he did not quite make it to the curb by the time I got to him. I had to swerve to avoid hitting the stooping man. As I passed, I realized who it was; we almost lost one of our best comedians. "

I guess I have my father to thank for putting a curse on the family. I've always hoped its true manifestation would never realized, which may be easier said than done in LA.

Traveling now on the 134, just before I passed signs for the Bob Hope Drive exit, I sped by the West Coast capital of NBC nestled among the infinite studios of Warner Brothers and Disney. Home to *The Tonight Show with Jay Leno*, the Burbank studio boasts the best local news with real stars as anchors: weatherman/comedian Fritz Coleman, who also served as honorary mayor of the neighboring community of Toluca Lake, carries the eleven o'clock news with starlet Colleen Williams and leading man Paul Moyer as anchors.

Yes, the NBC Studios are truly amazing for their modest size. Every time I drove by the line of people waiting to see a taping of *The Tonight Show*, I would honk and wave, you know, give them a thrill. But my affiliation to the studio, and the network, goes beyond just a thrill-giver to tourists.

My first direct encounter with the Peacock Network came when I was in seventh grade. I had always been a fan of the network that brought *Golden Girls* and *Diff'rent Strokes* to my television, but I became a part of the magic when I was thirteen. I got a call during dinner – as all calls usually come to my house – on a Thursday night.

After a short conversation with a deep-voiced woman, I had to ask for permission: "What do you think? Should I do it?" I asked my mom. "They want to know if I will come watch a new TV show and give feedback."

"What time? And are you sure this isn't just a solicitor?"

"A bunch of people in my class have gone or are talking about going. They *referred me*? I think it will be fun, but I am not sure? What should I do?"

"Do what's good for you," she said, as she always did.

Excited, I wrote down the information I needed for the following Tuesday. I went to school the next day in search of a classmate who would have, perchance, got called for the same day. It seemed as though just about everyone had been getting calls within that two-week period. I was relieved to know that two other girls, Nancy and Renee, were also going Tuesday afternoon.

I made sure I got all my homework done before my 4:30 "appointment." My mom dropped me off, yelling "good luck" at me as the van's sliding door slammed. She said she'd be back to pick me up an hour and a half later.

Nervous and excited, I approached the lobby, an anxiety knot almost fully developed in my stomach. I moved forward, though, knowing that the pain would go away as soon as I got situated and saw the girls that I knew. Familiarity.

Through the main entrance's double sliding doors, a woman sat at a standard concierge type desk sternly welcoming entrants. I told her my name as I uneasily looked around for the news "celebrities," but Colleen and Paul were nowhere to be found. The woman behind the counter pointed to the elevator and told me to go upstairs to a screen room. As I got into the elevator, I saw my friends and held the elevator for them as the knot in my stomach loosened. The doors closed, and Renee told a joke about being late (she claimed she was the funny one) – the loose knot unraveled into a string dangling from my sternum.

The room had a conference table with truly overstuffed chairs filled by other young people; we took the last three empty seats. A woman introduced herself – and told us to help ourselves to the snacks at the back of the room (and by snacks, she was referring to sandwiches, vegetables, fruit, cookies, cheese and crackers, and chips). She told us that everything from this point forward would be monitored, indicating red lights throughout the small room: the red eyes of the network.

The premise of the focus group was that we were to watch a pilot episode for a new series and then share our honest opinions. There was one last offer of food, then the lights dimmed, a TV screen lit, and the program began.

It started off with a catchy, upbeat theme song. Good start, I thought. I watched the 22-minute show, only laughing infrequently; it wasn't anything spectacular to me.

The lights came on, and the facilitator returned to start the discussion. "What do you think?" she asked. "What did you like? What didn't you like?"

A rather outspoken girl, whose nametag announced she was from Encino, was the first to speak. "I think it was funny, and I liked the way the guys and the girls all got along; it was cute, and I think that people will relate to a bunch of people like that — I mean, my friends and I hang out, and I think it's believable in that way." She kept going on about each character and their flaws and their personalities and their clothing choices. She had a lot to say – and she said it all. The facilitator took notes and affirmed each comment with "uh-huh" or "okay" or "I see."

She continued to pull opinions from the different viewers, but no answer was as longwinded as the first. When almost half of the group had shared, I finally felt comfortable enough to share my honest opinion, no strings attached.

"Well," I said. "It was okay. It started out good, but I think it's a lot like that show from last year, *These Friends of Mine*. I think TV is starting to get a lot of these kinds of shows." I started feeling even more confident as I spoke and the words seemed to flow on their own: "I don't really think this one will make it with all the others out there. The characters you have are okay, especially the blond one when she makes allusions to real things. And she has that mystical-type thing about her. She's a real different kind of character: A real 'character.'" There was no stopping me now: "But, honesty, though, I don't know how many people would watch a show about six friends who hang out at a coffee shop in New York – I just don't think people would really watch it. But that's just what I think."

Some others agreed with me; other disagreed. Fifteen minutes later, I got out of the elevator with two passes that never expire for a tour of the NBC Studios, ten dollars cash, and a feeling like I might have saved the network some money.

Three years later, humbled by the shows success, I went back to NBC to see a taping, but this time of the *Tonight Show*. Finally 16, Adam and I stood in line from almost eight in the morning to see Martin Short and the Red Hot Chili Peppers. The heat was intense, but we knew it would be worth it.

At about 5pm, we were almost to the front of the line, almost inside the building, almost through the metal detectors and able to see the *Tonight Show* set. I went through before Adam, handing my ID and a ticket for that night's show to the young attendant, who didn't even look 16 herself. Apparently, the studio had not forgiven me for my erroneous prediction for their show about friends; the young girl asked me to step to the side, and then she let Adam through and then people behind him.

Wearing his official burgundy blazer, her apparent supervisor came over and started asking me questions like, "Why do you want to see this show?" and, "How did you obtain your ticket?" and a bunch of other ridiculously pointless questions. Never had I gotten such a reaction for looking younger than I really was. I figured, if I'm old enough to stay up until 12:30 a.m. to watch the show, then I should be allowed in, regardless of how young I appear to be. Looking young might have gotten my mom a youth price at the movies until she was 23, but it's different now: I don't get the discount.

When I had sufficiently explained myself, satisfying his need for a secure audience, the hail of questions finally subsided; and he apologized about the inconvenience. He seemed satisfied that I was not going to disrupt the production of the show, so I asked if I could join Adam who had been passed through without incident.

Without making eye contact, he garbled his words, "I'm sorry, sir. It looks like we have filled the audience for today. I'm sure we could get you tickets for next week."

I didn't want to see next weeks' show; I wanted to see Martin Short and the Chili Peppers. Adam and I had been studying the "guest guide" for months planning on the perfect show to see. He again apologized and told me there was nothing he could do.

"Nothing? Are you sure you can't let me stand in an aisle or something?" I wasn't ready to give up; the taping was still over an hour away. "You've got to be able to do something."

As he politely began escorting me out into the inner foyer with me trying to convince him to let me see the taping, the door flung open, practically knocking me down. A gust of people merged by us and into the inner studio. The burgundy -coated man helped me up apologetically and then nervously got on his walkie-talkie and radioed someone in a muffled exchange.

"Sir," he said to me, grinning too largely, "it appears a seat has just opened up." He escorted me in and sat me in the front section of the audience. I wasn't' sitting with Adam, but at least I got to see the show.

The *Tonight Show* band started playing, and the producer explained the filming process. Finally, just before the show was to start, the producer made one final comment. "I want you all to have energy and enthusiasm when our announcer, Ed Hall, announces tonight's guests. And just so as not to catch you off guard, we've had to switch some guests around due to a booking snafu." Who says snafu these days? "Mr. Short has had to reschedule due to a problem with his car getting him here. We sent a limo, but the traffic is more than typical for the LA freeways." He laughed awkwardly. "And the Chili Peppers would be coming on, but Flea seems to have injured his hand."

Well, I guess all the hassle was worth it? Front row seats for a show that was not what I expected. The producer wasn't through yet, though:

"But don't worry folks, we have some great guest that graciously offered to come on tonight on such short notice. We have acrobats from Fox's recent "Greatest of Shows VI" and one of Jay's favorite standup comedians from the Comedy Store. But headlining tonight, we're excited to have a man you know from his comedy routines and his hit TV show: Jerry Seinfeld."

And the curse lives on.

THIRTY-SEVEN

With barely any traffic on the eastbound 134, I was easily able to leave the San Fernando Valley behind as I passed into the San Gabriel Valley. The last glimmer of light was fading in the west and lights started coming on along the freeway.

I had spent a lot of time in the Burbank area with Adam as we survived high school together. See, before we started driving, I was always over at his house swimming, playing video games, or watching a movie. When we wanted to have freedom from parents and get away from his house, we would just walk down the street to Bob's Big Boy.

We started frequenting Bob's just after it was registered as a California State Historic Sight and after DeNiro filmed a scene from *Heat* in a front booth. When we saw the plaques commemorating their respective events, we agreed that people would come more for the film credit than the historic value.

Bob's has great shakes, and being open 24 hours, we would end up there for a shake at any time. As the years passed, even after we started driving to El Cholo for green corn tamales instead of Bob's for a burger, we would go to the restored diner for shakes, sometimes both at 3 p.m. and 3 a.m. within the same 24-hour period.

Over shakes and fries, we would discuss girls we were pursuing and lament over those we could never catch. We'd talk of school and the future and how the two could co-exist. There was a shake for all occasions.

What I really liked about Bob's was that whenever we would go there with an issue to discuss, we never left until it was solved or severely analyzed. Like when there was finally success with a girl, we would stay and agonize over how to break it off because she was more insane than anyone realized. Or when we'd discovered how school figured into our futures, I'd push the subject as Adam tried to change it. We may not have always agreed on everything, but while at Bob's, the world was ours to pick apart and change.

I drove past Bob's and Burbank and headed out past Forest Lawn Cemetery. I was sailing right along, and then I was reminded of the Freeway Gods and the Dodger game that just ended. As I approached the interchange between the 134 and the 5, traffic came to a crawl. The left lanes were moving better than the right lanes that fed the 5, though by no means were they moving well. I think it would be safe to assume that the God of the 5 really likes home games at Dodger Stadium.

Going to a Dodger game is a quintessential Los Angeles experience, thanks to the O'Malley family, 60s architecture, Farmer John, and a little something borrowed (indefinitely) from Brooklyn. From Tommy Lasorda's glory days to the rise and fall (and rise again) of Hideo Nomo, I've seen some great baseball at Dodger Stadium. And no matter what the Giants or A's fans say up in the north, a Dodger fan is a real fan, too.

Home of the Farmer John "Dodger Dog," Dodger games are the best baseball has to offer. True, we may not have a stadium steeped in a century of history like those Back East, but we have a passion for the game that comes from living in LA. What's really great is being able to eat your way through nine innings, and no matter what section you are in, there's always someone near you that is either too drunk or too obnoxious (or both), which always makes for an unique experience that includes swearing, arguing, and the occasional removal from the venue.

And it's not just baseball and the refreshments that draw

people to the 1960s stadium. Musical performances have transformed the athletic arena into a performer's dream with 50,000 cheering fans: the ultimate validation. From the Beatles to Elton John, from Bruce Springsteen to The Three Tenors, performers know they've hit it big when they play the Stadium. Maybe that' why the Pope John Paul II likes LA – he's a Dodger fan, you know.

When the Pope came to LA in the '80s, I was too young to care. But my dad knew the importance of the pontiff, so he secured us a place to attend Mass at Dodger Stadium. Yes, Dodger Stadium is an athletic venue, a music venue, and an occasional Catholic church. We sat in the seats farthest away from the alter, I think, and I'm convinced we would have had a better view if we had stayed home and watched it on TV. Actually, by the time communion was offered to us, I think the Mass was over and the people seated on the field had already started to leave. But I guess by playing Dodger Stadium, the Pope knew he hit it big... and I don't think he took it lightly, either.

In order to be ordained a bishop, a priest friend of mine had to meet with the Pope in Rome. Upon his return, I wanted to know all about his papal encounter. He said he only saw the pontiff for a couple of minutes, but that he spoke to him about the blessing from god and devotion to the people.

"And when I told him I spent my life in Los Angeles," the new bishop shared with me, "He paused, looked at me, and in his thick Polish accent said, 'the Dodgers, they need to work on their fielding." The leader of the Catholic Church, the man attributed to the fall of Communism, a man who is said to have the closest connection to God – the Pope – is Dodger fan. Who can blame him? The franchise added to his notoriety here in LA.

After having been twice graced by presence of the Olympics, first in 1932 and then half a century later in '84, Los Angeles is a sports fan's dream (even without a professional football team). And though the glory days of the Olympiad have passed, we are still reminded by Olympic Boulevard and the occasional bumper sticker that reads, "I survived the LA Freeways in 1984." And if you are in Exposition Park and find yourself walking along behind the Coliseum at the back of the parking lot, I think the best sign that the Olympics have been in LA is the rusted, half-covered Olympic Rings that are taller than the small fast-food restaurant that they lean up against. Another treasure of LA's past just tossed away: where's the sportsmanship in that? Dodger Stadium never put the huge picture of the Pope with the masses out in the back of the massive parking lot.

THIRTY-EIGHT

Traffic moved slowly as cars from Dodger stadium continued to pile onto the 5. The lights from the Disney Animation Building at Disney Studios were still on as I passed the Sorcerer's Hat. I once heard that they have a gym, showers, and a big room with beds so that the animators could spend as much time as they needed to in the building creating a masterpiece. Then again, I've also heard that Walt Disney is cryogenically frozen and kept in a vault under The Pirates of the Caribbean ride. I am intrigued by Disney Magic.

Back in college, after a substantial paycheck from one of my summer jobs, I treated my self to an annual pass to Disneyland. Going at least once a month for the following 12 months, I realized Disneyland transcends the tangibles of "It's a Small World" and "The Enchanted Tiki Room" and instead becomes more of a theoretical state of mind. The physical changes to the park are slow and meticulous, but if you sit down and watch it all happen, month after month, the haze is lifted from Sleeping Beauty's Castle.

A couple of times, when school was getting particularly stressful, I would take the hour drive to Anaheim and spend an afternoon in the park. I'd bring books so I could get some work done, but I knew I'd probably ignore my bag of texts, using them as an excuse to sit and watch as the world unfolded on the street at the Main Street rotary.

Everyday, people come from all over the world to experience Disneyland, and if you "people watch," some things become glaringly obvious. Kids who go to the park today have a completely different experience than I had as a child, and I'm not talking about the change of attractions. Cell phones, walkie-talkies, and child leashes seem to take the thrill out of walking through the crowds. And if Disneyland is the self-proclaimed "happiest place on Earth," why are there always so many crying children and frustrated parents storming down Main Street to the exit?

Maybe it could be called, the "most romantic place on Earth," because couples seem to take every opportunity while in the park to kiss, cuddle, and make-out, whether waiting in line, on a ride, or just walking into the park. Or, maybe, 'the trendiest place on Earth," because Orange County's youth use the park as a hangout replacement for the mall. Or, "the most accepting place on Earth" might work, too: for some reason, it's okay to dress up like a fool while in the park, and everyone thinks you're the greatest. (Why can a 50-year-old dad wear a fluorescent pink tank-top that barely covers his enormous gut – which, mind you, is only being supported by a crushed, faded fanny pack – hold a balloon in one hand and a half-eaten churro in the other, wear Goofy ears and *still* think he looks "cool"?) Or perhaps the most fitting, regardless of the day or time you go: "the holiest place on Earth." Perhaps the Vatican has that one already, but I have never been to the park without seeing a group of nuns or monks or rabbis or some other clearly defined religious group.

Sometimes I wonder how life would have played out if Walt had built his theme park as he had originally intended. There is no doubt that Disneyland has helped define LA (and all of Southern California) from 40 miles away in Anaheim, but what would have happened if it was just over the hill in the studio-filled Burbank? Would the now flourishing studios of

Warner and NBC have moved to Glendale to the east or perhaps west to the aptly named Studio City? Would Burbank have become synonymous with Orlando? Burbank would not be the small town it appears to be today, that's for sure. Burbank's loss is Anaheim's gain – or is it?

When I finally passed from Burbank into Glendale, I was able to fly down the freeway. I passed through Glendale without incident, and then started making my ascent up the freeway towards Eagle Rock and then Pasadena.

By now, the crescent moon floated in the vast darkness with only an occasional defiant star with light enough to penetrate LA's atmosphere. Approaching the Eagle Rock, the actual geological formation for which the community was named, I looked to the right at one of the most beautiful sights from any LA freeway. When visitors comment how LA doesn't have any stars in the sky, I always nod in agreement and then explain that the stars in LA are on the ground: as you looked out over Eagle Rock and Glendale, with the Downtown skyline in the distance, the city sparkles with thousands of streetlights, porch lights, headlights, spotlights, and neon signs.

It takes thousands of twinkling entities to make the city shine, with or without the help of more heavenly bodies.

THIRTY-NINE

Now on the 210 eastbound, I finally drove the last few miles past the Rose Bowl, the Pasadena Playhouse, and Old Town Pasadena. The glowing lights along the freeway blurred as they passed, but none so spectacular as the view of just moments before. And upon entering Pasadena, you definitely know you've left Eagle Rock, the edge of the City of Los Angeles.

Pasadena is politically its own city like Beverly Hills or Palos Verdes, but it's still very much a part of LA and its culture. The aforementioned Rose Bowl, the Norton Simon Museum,

Old Town, and the Playhouse give Pasadena its charm, but the annual Tournament of Roses Parade has truly made the city bloom internationally. And for me, this annual event means more because of my family's own New Year's traditions.

My mother was born in Massachusetts, but as a five-year-old, her family relocated to "sunny Southern California" to help my grandmother recover from a bout with pneumonia. Across the country by train, her family traveled to a developing, orange grove-filled portion of Los Angeles: The San Gabriel Valley.

Recently, I have found myself being tied up in Pasadena for a number of reasons, both socially and for business. But for the first ten years of my life, Pasadena was my second home. At least weekly, James and I would visit my grandparents and often times spend the night. My grandmother was always taking us on errands that turned out to be adventures, too.

We three had an annual tradition, though, that seemed to be the biggest adventure of the year. Every year on the day after Thanksgiving, we would go to Stats – a huge Christmas-themed craft warehouse that was ahead of its time when I encountered it in the mid-eighties. The aisles were high, packed with indistinguishable holiday items, and always crowded with shoppers.

"Now boys," my grandmother cautioned to us every year as we walked down an aisle glistening from floor to ceiling with Christmas ornaments, "you can look, but don't touch *any*thing. I don't want to have to buy a broken ornament 'cause you dropped it. Understand?"

We both nodded in compliance every year. The last thing we wanted to do was make her angry (neither of us could forget her wrath the day we broke a terra-cotta pot in the backyard when we were doing her yard work). And each year, she would meticulously to pick through the bins filled with delicate ornaments.

One year, though, the aisle was unusually empty except for the three of us. We nodded in response to her annual warning and watched as she picked up a particularly ornate, and fairly expensive ornament.

"Isn't this beautiful, boys?" She held it up to us, and then...*CRASH!* She immediately cursed the ornament, the store, the aisle, the day, then gritted her teeth and said, "Come on boys, let's get out of here," as she grabbed us by the arms, digging her nails into my flesh, and then rushed us to a different aisle. My grandmother knew how to avoid confrontation.

Now, on the first of every year, her family would get up early to watch the Parade on TV, and then head to Craig Street and Colorado Boulevard to see the Parade in person. And when my mother grew up, got married, moved west to the Valley, and had her own family, she continued the tradition and would have us trek out to Craig and Colorado.

See, the tradition transformed as my siblings and I grew up, making it our tradition to watch the Parade on KTLA 5 with Bob Eubanks and Stephanie Edwards. Every year, I would wake to find my younger sister in front of the TV watching Bob and Stephanie commentate on the "floral pageantry" and "artistic arrangement of azaleas." I looked forward to my annual rendezvous with Bob and Stephanie and was reminded of it every time I saw Stephanie on a Lucky's commercial or Bob host a game show. And you know, I'm convinced that the writers of Disney's *Aladdin* based their parade commentators during the upbeat "Prince Ali" song on Bob and Stephanie. My New Year's would not be the same without them and KTLA.

Now, after seeing the Parade every year, one thing becomes strikingly obvious: the floats look awfully similar. Every year, it seems that the forms that are used – slightly altered and decorated differently – are remarkably reminiscent of the ones from the year before... and the year before that... and the year before that. Now, I know that they are not the same, but they sure do bear striking resemblance.

I also know they're different because I've helped build the floats since I was in eighth grade. Starting the day after Christmas, all over LA, floats are assembled for the Parade, but the majority is built in the vicinity of the Rose Bowl and Pasadena. Volunteers come and assist professional, paid float decorators and designers create floral masterpieces for a week, up until and through the morning of the Parade.

The intoxicating smell within the giant tents or warehouses where the floats are assembled overpowers even veterans on the first day of work. But as the week progresses, the industrial strength, floral glue fumes are barely noticeable, and the aroma and vibrancy of the flowers intensifies. My mom told me that I was merely adjusting to being high off glue fumes. And oddly enough, as I look back at the hours I volunteered, I could never remember being in a bad mood during any of them – maybe she was right.

After watching the Parade travel down Colorado, we would go back to my grandmother's house for lunch with all the relatives and celebrate the New Year with a Thanksgiving feast. Then, at about three o'clock, we would walk to the standing floats and view them up close as they posed in front of Pasadena High School. My visiting cousin, Carol, a florist who came each year from the Massachusetts, would identify all of the flowers, explaining which were rare or really expensive, and her "lecture/tour" would draw a small group who would listen as she walked from float to float. Sometimes, people would come up to us and ask questions, and Carol would matter-of-factly answer as if it was her job to do so, "Oh, yes. They are imported from Brazil." At dusk, we would walk back to my grandmother's – but the day was nowhere near being over yet.

After saying good-bye to our extended family, we would then drive over (just about a mile) to our Aunt's house. Now, she really was not my aunt; but she *was* my grandmother's best friend, and that qualified her to be called by *Auntie* Marge. She had three daughters, the oldest being my mother's best friend; but all the families were friends and called each other aunt, uncle, and cousin. Though completely unrelated to us, they were still family.

My mother had grown up with these girls, attending the same schools and church. My mother was the first to get married, so they were all in her wedding; and when it came time for the three sisters to get married, my brother and I were asked to be the ring bearers. ("What goes around comes around," as my dad always says.) Their family was very close to people who went to their church, especially those who lived in Pasadena. So when we arrived at their mother's house on New Year's Day evening, everyone who was there had grown up with my mother and had been her friend since before I was born.

The three girls lived in different areas now, but they all came home for the holidays and had a huge New Year's day party with everyone who grew up in the area, which now extended across the metropolis. Remember the Glum's, the ones who had stolen all the attention by getting engaged on the day I was born? They were there and always made a big fuss over our loose association.

"Oh, Benny," Mrs. Glum would say with a full smile, "we all screamed when you arrived. We were on pins and needles all night waiting for you. You took long enough to show up!" She'd retell the story every time new people came to the party. "I think that's why you're my favorite. And I mean that." She was very animated, a true high school drama teacher.

The bulk of the evening was spent preparing to eat, eating, cleaning up the food, and then eating again. I think my mother and her friends had a friendship based around food – which was fine with me. I have always tried to tell my friends that, instead of sitting around and trying to come up with something to do, we should just go and eat. More likely than not, we end up at a restaurant anyway, talking and laughing; so why not just go there from the start and spend a whole evening sharing good times and good food? That's the way to solidify any relationship: food.

Amidst all the food and frivolity, we never missed the "bowl games" that inundated the TV on New Year's Day. The men watched the games intently, while the woman and children moved between the game and the kitchen conversations. But everyone assembled in front of the TV for the halftime shows. And without fail, every year our favorite was the Orange Bowl Halftime Show.

"It's almost on! Come on!" One of the younger kids would shout from the TV room. We'd all rush in to see the start of the show that inevitably mixed pop culture, Americana, and hundreds of volunteer dancers.

"My goodness," my "aunt" would gasp and then start laughing. She was referring to the hundreds of dancers who were dancing to Gloria Gaynor's *I Will Survive* using aluminum foil-wrapped water bottles as batons.

"They've outdone themselves this year," her older sister (the self-proclaimed "smart one") said sarcastically as an Elton John-esque mob danced on a hydraulic stage draped with rolls of carpet, while two dozen Elvis Impersonators rocked out in front of a neon *Blue Hawaii* sign. The memories of that halftime show carry us through the entire year.

Hating to leave the fun and food behind, we were usually the last to say goodnight, always helping to clean up which included having a snack at about 9 p.m. from the leftovers we had just put away. The laughing would continue until we were in our car and driving away toward the 210 West.

Pasadena is where my grandparents have lived and worked their whole lives. Though an independent city, Pasadena's participation in LA culture goes beyond the fact that *The Sting* was filmed on its streets. Only from LA could come the Doo-Dah Parade, which graces the streets of Pasadena, mocking the Rose Parade with anyone willing to walk the route in absurd costumes and decorations. Downtown LA empties its 110 freeway into Pasadena, and I'm sure the Little Old Lady peels out on the 110 as she heads towards San Pedro. Pasadena is uniquely LA.

And today, as the white-suited Tournament Members on red mopeds escort the Parade past the Wrigley Mansion and then down Colorado Boulevard, I still listen to Bob and Stephanie's words and know what it is like to be there: on the floats, at the Parade, with my family, in Pasadena.

FORTY

Finally reaching my exit, Sierra Madre Boulevard, I moved to the right, knowing I was just a few miles from my destination. I started down the off ramp, and as I saw a sign indicating the miles to Azusa and San Dimas, I thought of how much time I spent in my car that day, how many miles I had driven, and how they both seemed to just fly by as my mind took to me to a thousand other times and places. By the time I reached the bottom of the off-ramp, I was thinking about how when I had kids, I wasn't going to let them buy ice cream from an ice cream truck: sometimes, my mind moves faster than I can keep up with.

I was only about two hours late for dinner, which probably threw my grandparents all out of whack. I had told them not to wait for me, but I am sure they had, worrying and arguing over why I was late. Just a few more minutes, and I could finally relax, and more importantly, they could relax.

As I sat at a red light at the bottom of the off-ramp, the Honda Civic in front of me blared rap music. It was so loud that I could actually identify the song, which was, oddly enough, Tupac's "To Live and Die in LA." I figured it was a young person like me, perhaps off to a relative's for dinner or coming back from a family barbeque in the Valley.

Sizing up the car, I looked to the license plate for some revelation about the driver. When I saw that this one was just a standard issue California plate, I strained to see what the unique license plate frame said. "The stars shine brighter in Truckee, California." I still remember to this day what it said because as I read it out loud, the car peeled out as it shot through the intersection. Almost immediately, a Pasadena Police cruiser – with full lights and siren – pulled the person over, though I'm not sure if it was because of the music or the skid marks.

I passed the scene slowly and realized that the driver was not a young kid. An older woman sat in the driver's seat, obviously upset that she had been detained. I guess I should have known it was going to be an older person because of the floral-decorated, school bus-yellow bumper sticker that read, "Jerry rode this bus." I smiled, imagining it meant Jerry Garcia. The woman was a deadhead.

I realize, now, my smile was premature. With just over a mile to go, I heard a rappling sound that, after ruling out a new backbeat to Gary Numan's "Cars," could only be flopping rubber: a flat tire. And sure enough, after I pulled to the curb and checked it out, I discovered that my right font tire had a rather large thorn in it. Except this thorn was different than ones I had encountered in my garden, as I looked closer – this thorn was metal and looked an awful lot like a giant nail.

Parked at the side of the road, I could barely see my tire. With its position against the curb, changing it there would be practically impossible. I could easily call the Auto Club and have them tow me somewhere, but that could take forever. I decided to just call my grandfather and have him come pick me up, and I could worry about it from their house, just a few minutes away.

I had passed a little corner market about a half-block back, so I figured I could walk to it and call from the pay phone out front. I reached back into my glove compartment for the collection of coins I keep there, and remembered, as I felt around for the coins, that I had used them all to pay for gas. All my coins and all my cash were gone. I sat down in the passenger seat and let my legs dangled into the street.

As I sat there, I thought about my day filled with extra expenses, added hassles, and extensive delays. I'm always up for an adventure, but this was verging on being ridiculous. I admit I'm no stranger to the out of the ordinary, but the day was more absurd than the time I drove around for three days with a Christmas tree on my car's roof because no one would take it to be recycled after January 15. (I unsuccessfully tried to convince my mom that leaving the decorated tree up as long as she could without it getting crispy, even if it lasted into February, wasn't a good idea.) For three straight days, I had to follow someone else's directions and leave the tree on my car because "it's too much effort to take it off and put it back on just so you can drive to school without a tree on your roof." This time, I was in control of the situation.

I wasn't going to sit there all night and sulk, and coins weren't going to fall from the heavens like manna into the desert. So, after one final look in every crevice of the car for a dropped quarter or dime, I knew what I had to do.

After one last, futile scavenge through the car for some tiny morsel, inkling or hint of money, I resolutely locked the car and started walking towards my grandparent's house. I could take care of things from there, and if worse came to worse, I could borrow one of their cars to take to work and deal with the flat in the daylight hours of the following day. So off I went, briskly walking to their house, the house in which my mother grew up.

I actually like walking, so this wasn't a challenge for me. And, usually, my walks weren't this short. I have been known to walk Wilshire Boulevard from end to end: downtown to the coast. And on an early Saturday morning, my friends know to find me walking through Griffith Park, 17 miles of trail leading nowhere and back. And every year, I retrace the steps of the first Angelenos, walking from Mission San Gabriel to Olvera Street, the original pueblo.

Sometimes I say that I take walks, but most times, the walk takes me. "Walk to clear your mind," my mother willfully suggests. When I walk, my mind is clearer, and usually allows a hundred new ideas to fill that newly vacated space.

I find that when I walk, I'm able to accomplish a lot, though. It's a great feeling to be able to say you walked 20 miles on a whim or got from the Valley to the beach without a car (and it might have taken just as long if you'd driven there via the 405). Even greater, though, is the freedom of thought when you are walking, eliminating the constraints of walls, structure, or even a car. The freedom of thought allows the freedom of solution.

While walking, I can change my course at in an instant and stop, pause, or detour for any reason. While walking, my mind controls my feet, and the street signs have no real power over them.

FORTY-ONE

Los Angeles is more than freeways. It's more than movie stars, gangs, trendy restaurants, and tourist traps; and it's more than the original Mulhollands and Chandlers could have ever envisioned. More than earthquakes and riots, more than beaches and the Rose Bowl, more than Dodgers and Lakers – LA is energy. It's more than you or I could even try to understand, even if we lived in the city our whole lives. Some, like you, might move away in frustration; others, like me, will stay on and try to make the best of it. To call LA your home allows you to view the world through smog-covered glasses, which isn't always a bad thing.

Don't worry - a lot of people hold on to the same ideas, myths, and untruths regarding life, people, and Los Angeles. A person can't be blamed for holding on to the beliefs that are perpetuated by a culture that clings to its past. But LA must be recognized beyond its civic boundaries.

In one of the last classes I took in college, a class on the futurist texts of Los Angeles, the professor presented works based in the present (and past) that extrapolated the worst of the city. *Bladerunner* was the main topic, as well as other texts that saw LA as the quintessential apocalyptic city. The professor argued that by its geographical position in the country on the Pacific Ocean, Los Angeles has the potential to disappear by self-inflicted wounds or by natural causes. We can't prevent the latter, yet most fear the former.

You know, we could focus on worrying, trying to prepare by building higher, thicker walls, or moving away altogether. Or, we can just take what we have and try to make it better. In the recent history of the over 200-year-old city, we've survived the earthquakes, El Niño, and even local news-named "Firestorms." We've survived self-inflicted wounds of civil unrest and the urban sprawl that extended the boundaries of the city over the horizon. We have something special, an unnamed energy that cannot be limited by the civic borders that Burbank, Torrance, Beverly Hills, or Long Beach have tried to use to separate themselves.

You know that the world's not perfect, but living in Los Angeles can give a person the ability to seek out and aspire toward perfection. I trust you to see the potential in the city, know that it exists to serve you and anyone else who allows the energy to guide them. Well, maybe not guide them, but to be a part of "the mix" that is LA. This is what you may still lack: openness to the possibilities of being alive. Without this, the city will look as bleak as Ridley Scott imagines.

As I walked along the street in the direction of my grandparent's little neighborhood, I was startled by a woman sitting on a step along the sidewalk. Normally, this wouldn't have made me even break my stride, but as I watched her, she became very familiar; something about her toothless smile was familiar. As I walked past her, I noticed on the other side of her was a wagon with a dog in it... and the dog was dressed in pajamas. I was caught off guard – could this have actually been the same woman I saw hours ago, just about ten miles away? It could have been, and I would have doubled back to see, but her excited and almost intoxicated warning to me truly consumed my attention as I walked by. As I approached, I heard her rambling to herself about "incorrigible youth." But as I walked past, she addressed me.

"Hey," she had said firmly with a fresh grin and a thick accent, "nobody walks in LA." Then she shouted, "I've got your number!"

I walked on quickly and chuckled to myself: "I do."

With about a block to go before turning onto my grandparents' little street, I was consumed in my quick-paced walk when the honk of horn startled me. I looked to towards the street and was blinded by headlights of an SUV, a red Explorer.

"Hey, there!" A woman's voice called out.

"Cindi? What are you doing over here? No Way." I was floored.

"Why are you walking? You know the rule?" she smiled as I leaned on her car door.

"What did you say?" It was so strange that she would say that. "Oh, forget it. Listen my car gave me problems and my cell broke and I ran out of cash and I'm trying to get to dinner."

"You wanted adventure." She smirked with care.

"Yeah, yeah, yeah. Can I get in?" By now, a few cars had swerved to avoid the parked car.

Apparently, Cindi had finished up a little later than she expected and came out to surprise me since she figured I'd be done eating by that point. She had left three messages on my phone, and figured, to catch me, she'd just come out to Pasadena. Lucky for me, she was driving as I was walking.

"You still up for those Tommy's burgers?" she asked.

"I gotta get to my grandparents – they're probably worried sick. They probably are starving, too, after waiting for me for hours. You know where they live, just up here, then left."

I probably should have just called my grandparents from Cindi's cell because when we finally got to their house, they didn't even realize I was late. They apparently had forgotten I was coming to dinner and had eaten hours before. They tried to push leftovers on me, but Cindi and I had declined in light of the plans we had made in the car.

"George," my grandmother said to my grandfather, "let the two of them go out." She turned to us, "Go have fun." And then to Cindi: "I hope we'll be seeing you again soon?" Every hint she dropped was as subtle as traffic on the Sepulveda Pass. Cindi and I looked at each other and smiled.

I left Pasadena in a heartbeat compared to the length at which it took to arrive there.

"I hope the freeway is moving – I'm starved," I said as I

leaned back in my seat and looked over at Cindi as we drove onto the 210 West.

"Well, we'll just have to see what your freeway spirits have to say about that," she smiled smugly almost winking at me.

"Gods. They're Freeway *Gods*." I couldn't help but smile, as my heart raced around my chest.

"Whatever," she said, looking back towards the freeway ahead and the city beyond.

About the Author...

Nobody Walks in LA is John Bwarie's premiere novel. A native Angeleno, he has lived in Los Angeles his whole life, save a brief stint earning a degree from the University of California San Diego. He has taught American Literature to high school students in Watts, worked as an Admissions Coordinator for a middle/high school, and spent time working for the community as a Los Angeles City employee. He continues to volunteer his time at local non-profits, especially those that promote literacy and motivate young people. He currently resides in LA's San Fernando Valley.

Commitment to the Community

"I believe that everyone has a responsibility to improve the condition of the larger community. As actions speak louder than words, I am committing my entire author royalty fee from the printing of this book (a percentage of the original purchase price) to education or community non-profit organizations. My goal is not to donate a large sum of money to just one or two organizations, but to assist many organizations with small donations for an immediate and specific need."

-J.B.

For more information on the author's "Commitment to the Community," please go to www.tdbooks.com

Acknowledgments

This book is in your hands because of the many people who were crucial in its creation and production. My editor, Anthony Fournier, was essential in keeping me on track and arguing a point until I realized he was right. The talented Matthew Goldman and Michelle Constantine were able to listen to my ideas and create an artistic reality far superior to what I had imagined. These three made the book what you hold in your hands now, but it started so much earlier...

Specifically, select teachers, instructors, and professors of mine made me think I could do this, from those in elementary school to college professors. I thank them for that motivation and also the realization that a good teacher encourages their students to follow their dreams, no matter how big.

Thanks must be given also to those others who, early on, read what I gave them and kept me going: Carol Abboud, Jean Abboud, Rose Abboud, Lou Berardi, Lisa Cernadas, Marc Chavez, Nikki Conis, Mike & Mark, Monique Farrah, Matt Henning, Adam Molina, Michelle Moore, Janice Saba, Martin Sanchez, Kathy Sayegh, The Shammas Sisters, Joseph Yoshitomi.

And then, there are the others who have contributed their own subtleties to the book and its formation: Scott Adams, Stephanie Andrade, Julie & Sam Alexander (& Marlene, too, for that plane ride and the title), John Arroyo, Missy Becker, Henry Bermudez, Favio Cacciagioni, Peter Ciulla, Colin Dehoney, Dustin Demont, Brendan Dixon, Jeff Dodge, Jessica Escobar, Cory Fitzgerald, P. A. Flaherty, Tom Gallagher, Juan Gomez-Quiñones, Megan Horton, John King, Sean Meyer, The Najim Brothers, Laura & Michelle, Dan Oster, The Sadd Siblings, Johnny Scalf, Bo & Trish Sharon, Linda Sharon, Kristi Shibata, Geoff Sloniker, Keith Tanner, Darius Wadia, Ryan Wertz.

And then, there were those who stood back and offered support and the urging to move forward; those are "the great encouragers": The Abuds, Neal Anderberg, Pat Anderson, Suzi Aparicio, Diane Aramony, Diane Arias, John Arroyo, Richard Barakat, G. Bennett, Patty Briles, Louis Choi, Logan DallaBetta, Katy Frengs, J.P. Ghobrial, Nancy Grohman, Julia Guevara, Mark & Cindy Haddad, Dana Izuhara, Phil Klain, David MacDonald,

Scott Mantell, Amber Montaño, Tom O'Neill, Tom Odell, Eamonn Oley, The Roum Girls, The S.J.'s, Pat Salvaty, Irene Saigh, Derek Smith, the staff at TMC, Gilbert Sunghera, Nancy Turner, Jerry & Cindy Yoshitomi.

Lisa Ball sat with me in our classes as we laughed at our instructors and, as we learned together, she made me feel like I could do this. This book would not have gone anywhere if she were not there for me as I thought of what might be.

Finally, my family was there for the creative process and let it all happen. From when I was young, my parents have encouraged me to take on new and challenging projects. They led my siblings and me to believe we could accomplish any goal we set forth to attain. This book truly would not be possible without them: they let me drive the streets and explore the world around me.

JOHN BWARIE
Los Angeles, 2003